rashi

RAMBAM

and

RaMaLaMaDiNeDoNe

✡ ✡ ✡ ✡ ✡ ✡ ✡ ✡ ✡ ✡ ✡ ✡ ✡ ✡ ✡ ✡ ✡

A QUIZBOOK OF
JEWISH TRIVIA FACTS & FUN

by

MARK D. ZIMMERMAN

Zimco Creative Arts, Inc.
Old Bethpage, NY

✡ ✡ ✡ ✡ ✡ ✡ ✡ ✡ ✡ ✡ ✡ ✡ ✡ ✡ ✡ ✡ ✡ ✡

ISBN 0-9644501-4-3

Library of Congress Control Number: 2003101804

INTRODUCTION

Jews are funny. All right, not every Jew. But lots of Jews are funny. We all know that many famous comedians are Jewish, from The Marx Brothers and Mel Brooks to Jerry Seinfeld and Billy Crystal. But not all funny Jews are famous. Take my Uncle Harry, for example. He's a Massachusetts Jew living in the heart of Cajun country. He tells jokes about Boudreaux and Thibodeaux, in his Boston accent. It doesn't get much funnier than that.

And why are Jews so funny? That, I can tell you in one word - TRADITION! (Okay, stop singing and pay attention). Jews have faced many hardships, from slavery in Egypt and the trek through the desert, to the Inquisition, pogroms, massacres, Nazis, and terrorists (I know, I'm losing you - after all, this is beginning to sound very unfunny. But be patient - I'm getting to the point). And how have we faced these hardships? With bravery, dignity, prayer, unity, and (here it comes), laughter. That's right - laughter is part of our tradition. Even in tragedy, Jews try to find a little room to laugh, to be reminded that there is a brighter side, a reason to keep going, a reason to feel good. And oftentimes, that reason comes from our sense of humor, our ability to laugh - at our enemies, and also, at ourselves.

Of course, besides being funny, Jews are also well-educated. The Talmud says that the education of children must never be interrupted, even to rebuild the Temple. That's why Jews are often called the People of the Book. (I'm kind'a hoping that in time we'll be called the People of the *Rashi, Rambam and Ramalamadingdong* Book). So put down your tools and get ready to be educated.

The trivia questions in this book are meant to test your knowledge about Judaism, and to help you increase your knowledge about Judaism. We've all been to that awful class where the teacher has a way of sucking the life out of any subject, leaving us drowning in our tears of boredom. In *Rashi, Rambam and Ramalamadingdong*, you can learn a little about Judaism without getting caught sleeping at your desk with drool running down the side of your face. Each question has one correct answer, as noted at the bottom of the subsequent page. But each question also has at least one answer designed to bring a smile to your face, and in some cases, maybe a chuckle, or, if you're reading while drinking, maybe even one of those snorts where the milk comes out of your nose. If none of the answers seem funny, or at least a bit clever, there are two possible reasons. One is that I failed, and in that case, you should just move on.

There are 219 questions and answers in the book – surely some of them will work for you. The other possibility is that I'm so clever that I fooled you. You know, like when everyone at the table is laughing at the private joke and you're not in on it. So you sit there with that half smile, trying to pretend that you get it, while hoping that they don't turn to you for some follow-up comments which will allow you to show your total ignorance. So before you reject a joke as not funny, ask a friend or relative (someone with a better sense of humor than you is recommended) if they get it. If they also can't find a reason to smile, send me an e-mail at *idonotgetthejoke@zimcocreativearts.com*. Tell me which question leaves you wondering, and I'll tell you why it's funny. Of course, at that point, it won't be funny, because even if it was funny when I wrote it, once you have to explain a joke it isn't funny anymore. But at least you'll be able to decide if you just missed the joke, or if I'm a complete idiot for writing it in the first place. Either way, I look forward to hearing from you.

Now, a little about the not funny stuff - that is, the stuff that is intentionally not funny. The trivia. All the correct answers really are correct, unless I screwed up, in which case I take full responsibility. Send an e-mail to *youscrewedthatoneup@zimcocreativearts.com* and tell me what's wrong. And regarding the age old question, "Who's a Jew?" here's how it works. In general, if a person is mentioned in the question, then he or she is a Jew, or at least a half-Jew (there are a few obvious exceptions - for example, in question #190, do I really have to tell you that Ho Chi Minh isn't Jewish?). People whose names appear in the answers may or may not be Jews. Sometimes, knowing who is and who isn't might help you figure out the correct answer. If you're curious about someone, e-mail me at *whoisthejew@zimcocreativearts.com* and I'll let you know.

There's an old saying that laughter is heard further than weeping. If you have anything else to say about this book, I'd love to hear from you. The laughter (your questions, suggestions, and positive reviews) should be sent to *iloveyourbook@zimcocreativearts.com*. The weeping (complaints, corrections, and negative reviews) go to *thisisnotareale-mailaddress@zimcocreativearts.com*.

FUNNY. EDUCATED. JEWS. These words just seem to go together like a horse and carriage. So that's why I wrote this book. It made me laugh, and it made me smarter. Hopefully it will make you laugh and make you smarter too. If not, you can't go for a ride in my horse and carriage!

ACKNOWLEDGEMENTS

Nobody other than myself had any direct role in the writing and production of this book (except the printer, and he already got paid - that's acknowledgement enough). But besides acknowledging myself, there are many whose influence enabled me to get to this point. I could list everyone who ever made me laugh, or taught me about Judaism, or taught me to laugh about Judaism, but the list would go on far too long. However, I couldn't proceed without specifically mentioning Groucho. While he was anything but religious, and though intermarried (When told he couldn't enter an exclusive club's swimming pool, he asked, "What about my son? He's only half Jewish. Can he go into the water up to his knees?"), his Judaism was part and parcel of his humor and personality. Anything ever said to him became a straight line for one of his puns, quips, or retorts. If anything I've written evokes even a hint of Groucho, then I've succeeded beyond my wildest dreams!

The portrait of Rashi on the front cover is by William D. Bramhall, Jr., and is used with permission from David C. Gross.

The portrait of Rambam on the front cover is courtesy of The Institute of Jewish Medicine and Moshe Rafael.

For giving me a purpose for everything I do, I thank my daughters Meryl and Melissa. I can only hope that I provide them even half the inspiration which they provide me.

For supporting me throughout, for proofreading, editing, questioning, suggesting, nudzhing, laughing, and being my best audience, I thank my wife Janet.

A. intentionally left blank.

B. for autographs.

C. left blank due to a printing error.

D. blank because some unwritten publishing law says you always begin the text of a book on the right hand page.

E. not really blank, it's your eyes.

Question #1: In addition to the Red Sea, what else was parted during the Exodus?

א: The Jordan River.

ב: The Euphrates River.

ג: The Yarkon River.

ד: The Dead Sea.

ה: Moses' hair.

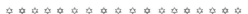

Question #2: Through what gate did the Israeli Defense Forces enter the Old City of Jerusalem during the Six Day War?

א: The Jaffa Gate.

ב: The Damascus Gate.

ג: The Water Gate.

ד: The Toll Gate.

ה: The Lion's Gate.

Question #3: What was the Pittsburgh Platform?

א: This was a proposal by the Jewish Federation of Pittsburgh to forbid spending money across the Green Line in Israel.

ב: A shoe with a very high heel, designed to allow women to see over the mechitza at the Young Israel of Pittsburgh.

ג: It is a small step stool, designed by a member of Congregation Ohev Shalom in Pittsburgh, to enable short Bar and Bat Mitzvah students to see over the lectern.

ד: A list of principles established by the Reform movement in Pittsburgh in 1885, including the abolition of kashrut rules.

ה: In 1868, a synagogue in Pittsburgh built a raised platform (bimah) in the front of the sanctuary, replacing the traditional table in the center of the room.

Question #4: For what was Chaim Nachman Bialik known?

א: He edited the daily prayer book that is commonly used in Orthodox synagogues in Israel.

ב: He was a renowned Hebrew poet.

ג: He invented the bialy.

ד: He wrote the first comprehensive modern Hebrew dictionary.

ה: He is the father of actress Mayim Bialik.

✡ ✡ ✡ ✡ ✡ ✡ ✡ ✡ ✡ ✡ ✡ ✡ ✡ ✡ ✡ ✡ ✡ ✡ ✡

Question #5: After whom was Netanya named?

א: Nathan Strauss.

ב: Benjamin Netanyahu.

ג: Natan Scharansky.

ד: Nathaniel Hawthorne.

ה: Tanya Harding.

✡ ✡ ✡ ✡ ✡ ✡ ✡ ✡ ✡ ✡ ✡ ✡ ✡ ✡ ✡ ✡ ✡ ✡

Question #6: To what does the term Golden Calf refer?

א: This refers to the ceremony which replaced animal sacrifices in the Temple. People would bring gold and jewelry, which would then be given to the poor.

ב: A sculpture outside the Knesset building, symbolizing Israel's rebirth in 1948.

ג: This was the name given to the first artificial calf given to an amputee at Hadassah Hospital in 1996.

ד: The ceremonial slaying of the first calf at the Jaffa stockyard, marking the beginning of the Israeli veal season.

ה: The golden idol constructed by the Israelites while waiting for Moses to return from Mt. Sinai.

Answers: #1 - א   #2 - ה   #3 - ד

Question #7: For what was Boris Pasternak known?

ת: He developed the process of pasteurizing milk.

ב: He was a Nobel laureate who wrote *Dr. Zhivago*.

ג: He was the arch enemy of Bullwinkle.

ד: He was a leader of the Russian refusenik movement, who was finally granted an exit visa in 1979, after 12 years in prison.

ה: He was a former member of the Soviet Politburo who later served in the Israeli Knesset.

✡ ✡ ✡ ✡ ✡ ✡ ✡ ✡ ✡ ✡ ✡ ✡ ✡ ✡ ✡ ✡ ✡ ✡

Question #8: In an Orthodox synagogue, what is the name of the divider between the men's and women's sections?

ת: The mechitza.

ב: The Wailing Wall.

ג: The mechina.

ד: The cone of silence.

ה: The peek-a-boo shmatte.

✡ ✡ ✡ ✡ ✡ ✡ ✡ ✡ ✡ ✡ ✡ ✡ ✡ ✡ ✡ ✡ ✡ ✡

Question #9: To what does the term Gezerah refer?

ת: A person from the Gaza Strip.

ב: The ceremony when priests ascend the altar during Yom Kippur services.

ג: At Sukkot, a ceremony when the carrots are harvested and blessed.

ד: A decree by the sages that something once permitted is now forbidden.

ה: In Kabbalist Judaism, a fatalistic view of the future, as in the song "Gezerah zerah, whatever will be will be."

Question #10: What is an Aufruf?

א: A private study session with the Rebbe in a Chassidic community.

ב: The calling up of the groom (and bride) for an aliyah before a wedding.

ג: A ceremony for thirteen year old dogs.

ד: A Yemenite wedding dance.

ה: The shofar blowing ceremony.

☆ ☆ ☆ ☆ ☆ ☆ ☆ ☆ ☆ ☆ ☆ ☆ ☆ ☆ ☆ ☆ ☆ ☆

Question #11: For what was Lily Solomon known?

א: She was one of the first women to fly a plane, drive a car, and ride a motorcycle.

ב: She was one of the first women to lay tefillin, wear a tallit, and read from the Torah.

ג: She was one of the first women to drive a sherut taxi, fly an El Al plane, and drive an Egged bus.

ד: She was one of the first women to slaughter a kosher chicken, perform a bris, and carve an ice sculpture at a bar mitzvah party.

ה: She co-founded Hadassah along with Henrietta Szold.

☆ ☆ ☆ ☆ ☆ ☆ ☆ ☆ ☆ ☆ ☆ ☆ ☆ ☆ ☆ ☆ ☆

Question #12: For what is Abraham Abraham known?

א: He was a rabbinic scholar who contributed much of the writing of the Mishnah.

ב: They are the Israeli version of the rock group Duran Duran.

ג: He co-founded, with Joseph Wechsler, the Abraham & Strauss Department Store.

ד: It is a novel about a family's struggles with racism, violence, and sacrifice in the south of Israel.

ה: He is the father of Isaac Isaac and Ishmael Ishmael.

Question #13: What is a Parochet?

א: A dumpling containing potato and spices.

ב: The person who holds the baby at the brit milah.

ג: The cup which holds water for the hand washing ceremony.

ד: The curtain which covers the ark.

ה: A device worn by Israeli paratroopers.

✧ ✧ ✧ ✧ ✧ ✧ ✧ ✧ ✧ ✧ ✧ ✧ ✧ ✧ ✧ ✧ ✧

Question #14: For what is Sylvan N. Goldman known?

א: He invented the shopping center.

ב: He invented the Home Shopping Network.

ג: He invented the shopping cart.

ד: His wife invented shopping.

ה: He is the founder of the Sylvan Learning Centers.

✧ ✧ ✧ ✧ ✧ ✧ ✧ ✧ ✧ ✧ ✧ ✧ ✧ ✧ ✧ ✧ ✧

Question #15: What are Ginnegar and Ginnosar?

א: The first Israeli test tube baby twins.

ב: The spices in the havdalah spice box.

ג: Two kibbutzim in Israel.

ד: The code names given by the Israeli intelligence agency Mossad to the Ashkenazic and Sephardic chief rabbis.

ה: The Hebrew names for the Tigris and Euphrates rivers.

---

*Answers: #10 - **ב**   #11 - **א**   #12 - **ג***

Question #16: Traditionally, who is the unseen guest at a bris?

א: The baby's mother.

ב: Isaac.

ג: Moses.

ד: Elijah the Prophet.

ה: Ralph Ellison.

✡ ✡ ✡ ✡ ✡ ✡ ✡ ✡ ✡ ✡ ✡ ✡ ✡ ✡ ✡ ✡ ✡ ✡

Question #17: For what is businessman Israel Matz known?

א: He is the founder of the Manischewitz Co.

ב: He founded the tourism company, Israel Welcome Matz.

ג: He is the founder of the Israel Matzah Co.

ד: He was the first owner of the New York Metz.

ה: He is the founder of Ex-Lax Co.

✡ ✡ ✡ ✡ ✡ ✡ ✡ ✡ ✡ ✡ ✡ ✡ ✡ ✡ ✡ ✡ ✡ ✡

Question #18: After whom was the Fourth Street Elementary School in Milwaukee renamed in 1979?

א: Harold Dorman, founder of Dorman's Cheese, which is located in Wisconsin.

ב: Golda Meir, who was a student there.

ג: Robert "Bud" Weiser, the first Jewish mayor of Milwaukee.

ד: Vince Lombardi, whose real name was Vincent Lomberg.

ה: Yitzhak Rabin, who went to graduate school at the University of Wisconsin-Milwaukee.

Answers: #13 - ד   #14 - ג   #15 - ג

Question #19: Who was Jeremiah?

א: The only adult survivor of a deadly plague which decimated the world, Jeremiah attempted to create a new and hopeful world.

ב: After the death of Moses, he led the Israelites into the Promised Land.

ג: A leader of the tribe of Issachar.

ד: The second of the major prophets.

ה: A bullfrog mentioned in the story of the ten plagues.

✧ ✧ ✧ ✧ ✧ ✧ ✧ ✧ ✧ ✧ ✧ ✧ ✧ ✧ ✧ ✧ ✧

Question #20: For what is Claude Lanzmann known?

א: He is a Nazi hunter who works with Simon Wiesenthal.

ב: The Claude Lanzmann are an organization of immigrants in Israel who are all originally from the village of Clauditchev in Poland.

ג: He is the filmmaker who made the film, *Shoah*.

ד: He designed the Israeli Holocaust Museum, Yad Vashem.

ה: He was the leader of the Warsaw Ghetto uprising.

✧ ✧ ✧ ✧ ✧ ✧ ✧ ✧ ✧ ✧ ✧ ✧ ✧ ✧ ✧ ✧ ✧

Question #21: What do Inbal, Batsheva, and Bat Dor have in common?

א: They are all Israeli cities.

ב: They are all traditional bat mitzvah songs.

ג: They are all Israeli dance companies.

ד: They are all enemies of Batman.

ה: They all had children who were fathered by King David.

Answers: #16 - ד   *#17 -* ה   *#18 -* ב

Question #22: For what is Bernard Baruch known?

 א: He wrote the daily prayer book, hence the many notations beginning with "Baruch Ata."

ב: He replaced Louis Brandeis on the United States Supreme Court.

ג: He converted from Judaism to Catholicism, and was later anointed St. Bernard.

ד: He was a financial advisor to four presidents.

ה: He was the second president of Israel, following Chaim Weizmann.

✧ ✧ ✧ ✧ ✧ ✧ ✧ ✧ ✧ ✧ ✧ ✧ ✧ ✧ ✧ ✧ ✧ ✧

Question #23: What are Nir Oz and Nitzane Oz?

א: These are the names of the first set of twins born in Israel after statehood was declared in 1948.

ב: These are the Arabic and Israeli versions of the HBO program, *Oz.*

ג: These are two villages in Israel.

ד: These are the names of the two tallest peaks in the Judean Mountains.

ה: They are the children of the Wizard of Oz.

✧ ✧ ✧ ✧ ✧ ✧ ✧ ✧ ✧ ✧ ✧ ✧ ✧ ✧ ✧ ✧ ✧ ✧

Question #24: What does Adon Olam mean?

 א: Lord of the universe.

ב: Guardian of the gates.

ג: Master of the house.

ד: Lord of the flies.

ה: Leader of the pack.

Question #25: What do Benzion Kapov-Kagen, Pinchus Pinchik, and Yosef Rosenblatt have in common?

א: They are all famous 20th century cantors.

ב: They all won the Eurovision song contest representing Israel.

ג: They all play in the Israel Philharmonic Orchestra.

ד: They are all members of the Backstreet Bochers.

ה: They are all winners of the annual Israeli polka contest.

✡ ✡ ✡ ✡ ✡ ✡ ✡ ✡ ✡ ✡ ✡ ✡ ✡ ✡ ✡ ✡ ✡ ✡

Question #26: What is a Wimpel?

א: A hamburger chain in Israel.

ב: A Torah binding made from the swaddling clothes of an infant.

ג: A nebbishy Jewish person.

ד: The processional when removing the Torah from the ark.

ה: A crying towel used at Jewish funerals.

✡ ✡ ✡ ✡ ✡ ✡ ✡ ✡ ✡ ✡ ✡ ✡ ✡ ✡ ✡ ✡ ✡ ✡

Question #27: What do we shake on the holiday of Sukkot?

א: Our booty.

ב: The greggar.

ג: The hands of the visitors to the sukkah.

ד: The lechem and egozim.

ה: The lulav and etrog.

Answers: #22 - ד #23 - ג #24 - א

Question #28: What do Joseph Kennedy, Nikita Khrushchev, Elvis Presley, and Chuck Connors have in common?

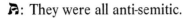

> **א**: They were all anti-semitic.
>
> **ב**: All worked as "shabbos goyim" when young.
>
> **ג**: They all sent congratulatory letters to Moshe Dayan after the Six Day War in 1967.
>
> **ד**: All attended Henry Kissinger's bar mitzvah.
>
> **ה**: All originally had the same last name - Cohen.

✡ ✡ ✡ ✡ ✡ ✡ ✡ ✡ ✡ ✡ ✡ ✡ ✡ ✡ ✡ ✡ ✡ ✡ ✡

Question #29: What false messiah converted to Islam?

> **א**: Elijah Mohammed.
>
> **ב**: Mohammed Ali.
>
> **ג**: Shabbtai Zvi.
>
> **ד**: John Walker Lindh.
>
> **ה**: Jacob Frank.

✡ ✡ ✡ ✡ ✡ ✡ ✡ ✡ ✡ ✡ ✡ ✡ ✡ ✡ ✡ ✡ ✡ ✡ ✡

Question #30: What do Lionel Tiger, Marcel Mauss, and Eric Wolf have in common?

> **א**: They are all signers of the Israeli Declaration of Independence.
>
> **ב**: All are characters on the Israeli version of *Sesame Street, Rechov Sumsum.*
>
> **ג**: They can all be found at the Biblical Zoo in Jerusalem.
>
> **ד**: All served as United States ambassadors to Israel.
>
> **ה**: They are all noted anthropologists.

Answers: #25 - א   #26 - ב   #27 - ה

Question #31: A unit of measurement was named after what famous Jew?

א: Ezra Pound.

ב: Heinrich Hertz.

ג: Dorothy Kilgallen.

ד: Harold Pinter.

ה: Ted Bessel.

☆ ☆ ☆ ☆ ☆ ☆ ☆ ☆ ☆ ☆ ☆ ☆ ☆ ☆ ☆ ☆ ☆

Question #32: Who are the Maskilim?

א: Disciples of Maimonides.

ב: Those who accepted the Enlightenment, known as the Haskalah.

ג: They were followers of Rabbi Moshe of Ashkelon, known as the Maskil Rebbe.

ד: An organization of Israelis who originally come from Moscow.

ה: People who dress up for Purim.

☆ ☆ ☆ ☆ ☆ ☆ ☆ ☆ ☆ ☆ ☆ ☆ ☆ ☆ ☆ ☆ ☆

Question #33: What is Tallit Katan?

א: A small, four-cornered garment worn under the clothes.

ב: A prayer shawl, made of cotton.

ג: A prayer shawl, worn only by unmarried males.

ד: A prayer shawl, designed for people under five feet tall.

ה: The Jewish name of *Saturday Night Live* news anchor Kris Kattan.

Question #34: Who donated the money for the Bunker Hill monument?

א: Judah P. Benjamin.

ב: Judah Touro.

ג: Uriah P. Levy.

ד: Benny Hill.

ה: Carroll O'Connor.

✧ ✧ ✧ ✧ ✧ ✧ ✧ ✧ ✧ ✧ ✧ ✧ ✧ ✧ ✧ ✧ ✧

Question #35: What is the I.D.F.?

א: The Israel Dance Forum, an annual dance competition featuring Jewish dance troupes from around the world.

ב: The Israeli Diamond Foundation, which oversees all diamond processing operations in Israel.

ג: The Israel Defense Forces.

ד: The International Daveners Fund, a charity which supports Jews who pray at the Western Wall on a full time basis.

ה: The Illegal Dining Federation, a group of Orthodox Israelis who secretly meet at non-kosher restaurants to eat.

✧ ✧ ✧ ✧ ✧ ✧ ✧ ✧ ✧ ✧ ✧ ✧ ✧ ✧ ✧ ✧ ✧

Question #36: What is the Arbeter Ring?

א: A skin ailment, caused by eating meat and milk together.

ב: A ring around Mars, which can only be seen from Jerusalem.

ג: The ring traditionally given to a bride at her wedding.

ד: The Workmen's Circle organization.

ה: During hakafot, the ring of people dancing around the sanctuary.

Question #37: What playwright wrote "The Bald Prima Donna"?

ה: Sy Sperling.

ב: Arthur Miller.

ג: Eugene Ionesco.

ד: David Rabe.

ה: Sinead O'Connor.

✡ ✡ ✡ ✡ ✡ ✡ ✡ ✡ ✡ ✡ ✡ ✡ ✡ ✡ ✡ ✡ ✡ ✡

Question #38: What is the Aggadah?

ה: That part of the Talmud which includes legends and descriptions of historical events.

ב: The Haggadah, as it is referred to in England.

ג: Refers to the ark carried by the Israelites through the desert.

ד: The traditional Passover song *One Kid*.

ה: Refers to the biblical story of G-d's command to Abraham to sacrifice his son Isaac.

✡ ✡ ✡ ✡ ✡ ✡ ✡ ✡ ✡ ✡ ✡ ✡ ✡ ✡ ✡ ✡ ✡ ✡

Question #39: After whom was Zichron Yaakov named?

ה: The biblical Jacob, son of Isaac.

ב: The father of Baron Edmond de Rothschild.

ג: Yaakov Smirnoff, who was the first comedian to perform at the Comedy Club in Tel Aviv.

ד: Rabbi Yaakov Yosef, a disciple of the Baal Shem Tov, whose work *Toledot Yaakov Yosef* was the first book to be published by Chassidim.

ה: This is the Hebrew name of Ziggy Stardust.

Answers: #34 - ב   *#35 -* ג   *#36 -* ד

Question #40: What is Cantillation?

ה: Getting the cantor excited.

ב: The annual concert of cantors in Israel.

ג: The term originally applied to the mode of chanting or intonation used in the public recital of prayers and holy scripture.

ד: The celebration held by soldiers in the Israel Defense Forces when they complete basic training.

ה: The name of the trope (musical notation) used when reading the Megillat Esther.

☆ ☆ ☆ ☆ ☆ ☆ ☆ ☆ ☆ ☆ ☆ ☆ ☆ ☆ ☆ ☆ ☆ ☆ ☆

Question #41: What is Canaan?

ה: Abel's first name.

ב: The biblical land promised by G-d to Abraham.

ג: The capital city of Judea.

ד: The biblical land east of Judea and Samaria.

ה: The land where Moses died when he was not allowed to enter the Promised Land.

☆ ☆ ☆ ☆ ☆ ☆ ☆ ☆ ☆ ☆ ☆ ☆ ☆ ☆ ☆ ☆ ☆ ☆

Question #42: What French actress was nominated for best actress in 1966?

ה: Anouk Aimee.

ב: Bridget Bardot.

ג: Catherine Denieuve.

ד: Fifi Fofum.

ה: Simone Signoret.

Question #43: What do Eric Berne, Erik Erikson, and Erich Fromm have in common?

א: They are all Nobel prize winners for economics.

ב: They are all famous psychologists.

ג: They are all presidents of universities in the United States.

ד: They are all noted singers who have performed with the Israel Opera Company.

ה: They are all members of the cantorial group, *The Singing Ericks*.

✧ ✧ ✧ ✧ ✧ ✧ ✧ ✧ ✧ ✧ ✧ ✧ ✧ ✧ ✧ ✧ ✧ ✧

Question #44: What is Haganah?

א: A woman who is unable to remarry because her husband has not granted her a religious divorce.

ב: The processional with the Torah scrolls which takes place on Simchat Torah.

ג: The lifting of the Torah at the end of the Torah reading.

ד: An Israeli dance, usually performed to the song, *Haganah Gila*.

ה: The secret organization founded in 1920 to protect the Jewish population in Palestine.

✧ ✧ ✧ ✧ ✧ ✧ ✧ ✧ ✧ ✧ ✧ ✧ ✧ ✧ ✧ ✧ ✧ ✧

Question #45: For what is Albert "Dolly" Stark known?

א: He was the first Jew to win the Heisman trophy.

ב: A rabbinical scholar who always asked "Lama" ("Why," in Hebrew), he became known as the Dolly Lama.

ג: He was a major league baseball umpire.

ד: He was the person about whom the play *Hello Dolly* was written.

ה: He was the first coach of the Yeshiva University basketball team.

Question #46: For what are Marla Rosenfeld Barugel and Erica Lippitz known?

א: They are the first two female graduates of the Cantorial School of the Jewish Theological Seminary.

ב: They are the first two Israelis to win medals at the Olympic games.

ג: These are the real names of Marla Maples and Ivana Trump.

ד: They are the first two Jewish women to serve in the United States House of Representatives.

ה: They are the first Jews to win *Survivor*.

✿ ✿ ✿ ✿ ✿ ✿ ✿ ✿ ✿ ✿ ✿ ✿ ✿ ✿ ✿ ✿ ✿ ✿ ✿

Question #47: What group in the Bible refused to cut their hair?

א: The Jebusites.

ב: The Nazirites.

ג: The Hittites.

ד: The Hippyites.

ה: The Sheitelites.

✿ ✿ ✿ ✿ ✿ ✿ ✿ ✿ ✿ ✿ ✿ ✿ ✿ ✿ ✿ ✿ ✿ ✿

Question #48: What do James Schlesinger, Michael Blumenthal, and Arlo Guthrie have in common?

א: All have recorded versions of *The City Of New Orleans*.

ב: All are the children of famous folk singers.

ג: All converted to Christianity from Judaism.

ד: To celebrate the reunification of Jerusalem, they all shared a kosher Thanksgiving dinner at Alice's Glatt Bar in Jerusalem in 1967.

ה: All were advisors to President Jimmy Carter.

Question #49: Who was Obadiah?

♪: Fourth of the twelve minor prophets.

♫: A character in the Beatles song *Obadiah Obadah.*

♩: The wife of Jeremiah the prophet.

♭: Obadiah ben-Master was the Rebbe of the Yeshivat Geisand-dolz in Poland.

♯: A bullfrog mentioned in the story of the ten plagues.

✧ ✧ ✧ ✧ ✧ ✧ ✧ ✧ ✧ ✧ ✧ ✧ ✧ ✧ ✧ ✧

Question #50: What is Rashbam?

♪: This is the name that Sephardic Jews use to refer to Rashi.

♫: A skin disease, cured by bathing in the Dead Sea.

♩: Nickname for Samuel ben Meir, a French scholar, grandson of Rashi.

♭: A Spanish scholar, Yosef ben Moshe, grandson of Rambam.

♯: A Polish scholar, Rozanne ben Zannadanna, grandson of Ramalamadingdong.

✧ ✧ ✧ ✧ ✧ ✧ ✧ ✧ ✧ ✧ ✧ ✧ ✧ ✧ ✧ ✧

Question #51: For what is Harry Ritz known?

♪: He founded the Ritz Hotel.

♫: He invented Ritz Crackers.

♩: He threw such an elaborate bar mitzvah party for his son that as a result, the word "ritzy" was coined.

♭: He was a fighter pilot for the United States in World War II who went on to start the Haganah Air Force in 1947.

♯: He was one of the members of the Ritz Brothers comedy team.

Answers: #46 - ♪   #47 - ♫   #48 - ♩

Question #52: For what is Isaac Abrabanel known?

א: He founded the Bali Brassiere Co.

ב: To Sephardic Jews, this is the Ladino name of Isaac, meaning Isaac, son of Abraham.

ג: He was the first chief rabbi of Israel.

ד: He was an advisor to King Ferdinand and Queen Isabella.

ה: He was a mystic from Zefat (Safed) who coined the phrase "abracadabra."

✡ ✡ ✡ ✡ ✡ ✡ ✡ ✡ ✡ ✡ ✡ ✡ ✡ ✡ ✡ ✡ ✡

Question #53: What is Caesarea?

א: An ancient Mediterranean town, known today for its reconstructed amphitheater.

ב: The Roman ruins uncovered at Megiddo.

ג: A common stomach disorder in Israel, caused by eating salad with rancid Italian dressing.

ד: The city where the Romans established their headquarters after conquering Israel in the year 73 c.e.

ה: A holiday celebrated by Italians commemorating the Roman conquest of Masada.

✡ ✡ ✡ ✡ ✡ ✡ ✡ ✡ ✡ ✡ ✡ ✡ ✡ ✡ ✡ ✡ ✡

Question #54: What happens in the Jubilee Year?

א: Sacrifices are brought to the Temple in Jerusalem.

ב: Slaves are freed and land is returned to its original owner.

ג: The cherries are harvested on Israeli kibbutzim.

ד: All debts are forgiven.

ה: Fields are left fallow.

Question #55: To what does Red Heifer refer?

א: The breed of cattle which is used to produce Chalav Yisrael.

ב: The original name of Red Auerbach.

ג: The Druse equivalent of the Israeli Red Magen David and the Arabic Red Crescent.

ד: The Communist party of Haifa.

ה: A red calf, sacrificed in biblical times for its ashes, which when mixed with water could remove the impurity resulting from contact with the dead.

✧ ✧ ✧ ✧ ✧ ✧ ✧ ✧ ✧ ✧ ✧ ✧ ✧ ✧ ✧ ✧ ✧

Question #56: For what is Arthur Syzk known?

א: He designed the scroll used for Israel's independence proclamation.

ב: He was the first conductor of the Israel Philharmonic Orchestra.

ג: He wrote *Hatikvah*.

ד: He founded the Syzk Razor Company.

ה: He is the only rabbi in America whose name contains a *y* followed by a *z*.

✧ ✧ ✧ ✧ ✧ ✧ ✧ ✧ ✧ ✧ ✧ ✧ ✧ ✧ ✧ ✧ ✧

Question #57: What is Sepphoris?

א: A biblical venereal disease.

ב: A ceremony of sacrifice in the Temple in Jerusalem.

ג: An ancient city in the Galilee.

ד: What the Israelites in the desert couldn't see for setrees.

ה: A city in northern Israel known for its connection to mystical Judaism.

Question #58: For what is Dov Heller known?

א: He was raised as a Reform Jew, converted to Christianity, was
ordained a Presbyterian minister, and then later became an
ordained Orthodox rabbi.

ב: He was born a Palestinian Arab, married a Catholic woman, and
became a member of the Israeli parliament.

ג: He was born a woman, underwent a sex change operation, and
won the men's diving competition at the Maccabean games.

ד: He was born Steven Katz, recorded folk songs as Cat Stevens,
converted to Islam as Mahmoud Al-salaam, and won the Chassidic
song festival in 1988.

ה: He wrote the novel, *Catch-22*.

✧ ✧ ✧ ✧ ✧ ✧ ✧ ✧ ✧ ✧ ✧ ✧ ✧ ✧ ✧ ✧ ✧ ✧

*Question #59: What instrument is used to make noise when the name of
Haman is read on Purim?*

א: A hamanica.

ב: A greggar.

ג: A shofar.

ד: A lyre.

ה: A timbrel.

✧ ✧ ✧ ✧ ✧ ✧ ✧ ✧ ✧ ✧ ✧ ✧ ✧ ✧ ✧ ✧ ✧ ✧

Question #60: What is Sumer?

א: The season before Fal.

ב: The city at the base of Mt. Sinai.

ג: The senior senator from New York.

ד: The southern region of Babylonia.

ה: The biblical name for Syria.

Question #61: What does Besamim refer to?

א: Spices, such as those used during havdalah.

ב: The branches placed on the roof of the sukkah.

ג: A Ladino song - "Besamim, besamim mucho."

ד: The silver filials placed on top of the Torah scroll.

ה: The name of the cemetery where David ben-Gurion is buried.

✡ ✡ ✡ ✡ ✡ ✡ ✡ ✡ ✡ ✡ ✡ ✡ ✡ ✡ ✡ ✡ ✡

Question #62: What is Vulgate?

א: A 2nd century scandal when Jews began to follow the Roman god Vulcan.

ב: The southern entrance to the Old City of Jerusalem.

ג: The name of the code of laws written by Maimonides.

ד: An Israeli birth control product.

ה: A fourth century Latin translation of the Bible.

✡ ✡ ✡ ✡ ✡ ✡ ✡ ✡ ✡ ✡ ✡ ✡ ✡ ✡ ✡ ✡ ✡

Question #63: For what is Joseph Hertz known?

א: He coined the UJA phrase, "Give 'til it hertz."

ב: He founded Hertz Rent-a-Car.

ג: He was chief rabbi of the British Commonwealth, and wrote a famous commentary on the Torah.

ד: He was one of the founders of the Jewish Theological Seminary.

ה: He founded the Israeli city of Hertzliyah.

Answers: #58 - א   #59 - ב   #60 - ד

Question #64: For what is Mordecai Noah known?

א: He is a cult leader in Israel who claims to be the reincarnation of Mordecai and Noah. His followers are filling an ark with two of each kind of hamantashen.

ב: He was the first chief rabbi of Israel.

ג: He was the first Jew appointed to a high United States diplomatic post.

ד: Rabbi Mordecai Noah, known as the Ramnah, was an early Chassidic leader.

ה: He was a false Messiah in 17th century Poland who eventually converted to Christianity.

☆ ☆ ☆ ☆ ☆ ☆ ☆ ☆ ☆ ☆ ☆ ☆ ☆ ☆ ☆ ☆ ☆ ☆ ☆

Question #65: What is a Mohel?

א: Tzeitel's husband, the tailor Mohel Kamzoil.

ב: The one who performs the brit milah, the circumcision.

ג: A small blemish on the face.

ד: The person who holds the baby at a brit milah.

ה: A small non-kosher mammal found in the Negev Desert.

☆ ☆ ☆ ☆ ☆ ☆ ☆ ☆ ☆ ☆ ☆ ☆ ☆ ☆ ☆ ☆ ☆ ☆ ☆

Question #66: What is a Citron?

א: An etrog, a lemon-like fruit, which is one of the four species used on Sukkot.

ב: A French car popular in Israel.

ג: This refers to the adornment on the top of the Torah scroll handles.

ד: The special white yarmulke worn by the cantor only on Yom Kippur.

ה: A type of candle which keeps mosquitoes away from a sukkah.

Question #67: What do Henry Heller, Abraham Cohn, Benjamin Levy, and David O'Branski have in common?

א: They were all Jewish members of the House of Representatives during the Nixon administration.

ב: They are all members of the Klezmer Conservatory Band.

ג: These are the real names of the Marx Brothers.

ד: They were members of the vaudeville comedy troupe, "3 Yids and a Goy."

ה: They were all Jews who won the Congressional Medal of Honor during the Civil War.

✡ ✡ ✡ ✡ ✡ ✡ ✡ ✡ ✡ ✡ ✡ ✡ ✡ ✡ ✡ ✡ ✡ ✡

Question #68: What is a Blech?

א: What an Orthodox Jew says when he discovers that he accidentally ate treif.

ב: The tie which is wrapped around the Torah scroll.

ג: A Yemenite dance.

ד: The knife used by a mohel in a circumcision.

ה: A hot plate used for keeping food warm on the Sabbath.

✡ ✡ ✡ ✡ ✡ ✡ ✡ ✡ ✡ ✡ ✡ ✡ ✡ ✡ ✡ ✡ ✡ ✡

Question #69: To whom was the Balfour Declaration written?

א: Benjamin Disraeli.

ב: David ben-Gurion.

ג: Lord Rothschild.

ד: Jim Bouton.

ה: Dear Abby.

Answers: #64 - ג   #65 - ב   #66 - א

Question #70: What record was set by El Al Airlines on a flight from Montreal to Tel Aviv on March 26, 1984?

א: It was the first trans-Atlantic commercial flight by a twin-engine plane.

ב: A record was set for the number of bagels served on a non-stop flight.

ג: The flight contained the largest number of Canadians ever to make aliyah in one day.

ד: It contained the largest minyan ever held at 30,000 feet.

ה: Because the flight contained over a hundred Orthodox Jews going on a mission, it was the first flight to ever have a mechitza placed down the center aisle, separating the men from the women.

✡ ✡ ✡ ✡ ✡ ✡ ✡ ✡ ✡ ✡ ✡ ✡ ✡ ✡ ✡ ✡ ✡

Question #71: What is a Kess?

א: Something Jewish boys and girls give each other on the leps.

ב: The glass that is broken by the groom at a wedding.

ג: A spiritual leader within the Ethiopian Jewish community.

ד: The fur hat favored by some Chassidic Jews.

ה: The name of the pointer used during the Torah reading.

✡ ✡ ✡ ✡ ✡ ✡ ✡ ✡ ✡ ✡ ✡ ✡ ✡ ✡ ✡ ✡ ✡

Question #72: To feed the Israelites in the desert, G-d sent them a form of dew which tasted like wafers made with honey. What was this called?

א: Omer.

ב: Graham Crackers.

ג: Mandelbrodt.

ד: Latkes.

ה: Manna.

Answers: #67 - ה   #68 - ה   #69 - ג

Question #73: To what does Aljamas refer?

א: This is a Palestinian group dedicated to the destruction of Israel.

ב: This refers to the sacrifices made by the priests in the Temple.

ג: Night clothes worn by religious Jews.

ד: The Jewish quarters in Sephardic lands.

ה: The evening prayers of Muslims.

✿ ✿ ✿ ✿ ✿ ✿ ✿ ✿ ✿ ✿ ✿ ✿ ✿ ✿ ✿ ✿ ✿

Question #74: What do Felix Bloch and Konrad Bloch have in common?

א: Both won the Nobel prize, Felix for physics, and Konrad in physiology and medicine.

ב: They were an early Borscht Belt comedy act known as "The Bloch Heads."

ג: Felix, a rabbi, and Konrad, a cantor, were the first brothers to share a pulpit in the same congregation in the United States, at Congregation Tifereth Israel in Philadelphia.

ד: They both served in the United States Senate.

ה: They are the first gay Jewish couple to have their story printed in the *New York Times's* "Weddings and Celebrations" section.

✿ ✿ ✿ ✿ ✿ ✿ ✿ ✿ ✿ ✿ ✿ ✿ ✿ ✿ ✿ ✿ ✿

Question #75: What is the name for the rollers to which the Torah scroll is attached?

א: Etz Chaim.

ב: Rimonim.

ג: Mitzvah sticks.

ד: The hagbah (left roller) and the g'lilah (right roller).

ה: Holy rollers.

Question #76: Who was Phillip Klutznick?

א: An Israeli Shabbat morning cartoon character.

ב: The American ambassador to Israel.

ג: A community planner, diplomat, and president of B'nai B'rith.

ד: A character from the *Saturday Night Live* skit "The Klutznicks Of Kleveland."

ה: The executive director of the American Israel Public Affairs Committee.

✡ ✡ ✡ ✡ ✡ ✡ ✡ ✡ ✡ ✡ ✡ ✡ ✡ ✡ ✡ ✡ ✡

Question #77: Who is responsible for designing and building the George Washington, Verrazzano, and Triboro Bridges in New York?

א: Lloyd Bridges.

ב: Milton Steinberg.

ג: George Verrazzano, III.

ד: David Steinman.

ה: George Steinbrenner.

✡ ✡ ✡ ✡ ✡ ✡ ✡ ✡ ✡ ✡ ✡ ✡ ✡ ✡ ✡ ✡ ✡

Question #78: To what did Betty Perske and Shimon Perske change their names?

א: Barbra Streisand and Hal Prince.

ב: Bert Parks and Shelly Winters.

ג: Lauren Bacall and Shimon Peres.

ד: Betty Boop and Simon Says.

ה: Pearl Bailey and Pearl Jam.

Question #79: For what was Emile Berliner known?

ℵ: He was an inventor who did pioneering work in such areas as phonographs, long distance telephone communication, and helicopter design.

ℶ: He was the leader of the Warsaw Ghetto revolt.

ℷ: He was the presidential script writer who wrote the quote uttered by John Kennedy at the Berlin Wall, "Ich bin ein Berliner."

ℸ: He was the first Reform rabbi ordained in the United States.

E: He wrote the famous "J'accuse" letter in response to the trial of Captain Alfred Dreyfus.

✡ ✡ ✡ ✡ ✡ ✡ ✡ ✡ ✡ ✡ ✡ ✡ ✡ ✡ ✡ ✡ ✡

Question #80: What is Carole King's real name?

ℵ: Carole Melech.

ℶ: Carrie Nation.

ℷ: Carol Klein.

ℸ: Carol Koenig.

E: Coretta Scott King

✡ ✡ ✡ ✡ ✡ ✡ ✡ ✡ ✡ ✡ ✡ ✡ ✡ ✡ ✡ ✡ ✡

Question #81: Who is Yosef Caro?

ℵ: A Spanish codifier who edited the *Shulchan Arukh*.

ℶ: The founder of the city of Cairo.

ℷ: The inventor of Caro Syrup.

ℸ: A Jewish historian in ancient Babylonia.

E: Nicknamed the Yoko, he was a biblical scholar in 16th century Russia.

Answers: #76 - ℷ   #77 - ℸ   #78 - ℷ

Question #82: Who wrote "Jerusalem Of Gold"?

א: Naomi Shemer.

ב: Geula Gil.

ג: Goldie Hawn.

ד: Golda Meir.

ה: Bob Dylan.

✿ ✿ ✿ ✿ ✿ ✿ ✿ ✿ ✿ ✿ ✿ ✿ ✿ ✿ ✿ ✿ ✿ ✿ ✿

Question #83: What is Bimah?

א: Part of a song - "Bimah, bimah baby."

ב: The Hebrew word for ark, referring to Noah's ark.

ג: The pulpit in a synagogue.

ד: A foreign car popular in Israel, also called BMW.

ה: The curtain on the ark.

✿ ✿ ✿ ✿ ✿ ✿ ✿ ✿ ✿ ✿ ✿ ✿ ✿ ✿ ✿ ✿ ✿ ✿ ✿

Question #84: What is the Bund?

א: A buckle, part of the ceremonial clothes worn by religious men at their weddings. The bund is combined with a cloth belt called the cummer, forming the cummerbund.

ב: The Jewish Socialist Party, founded in Vilna in 1897.

ג: Refers to the central square of the ghetto where Jews would gather and share news.

ד: In the Chassidic community the Bund is the central organization that coordinates the distribution of charity.

ה: The code name used for the head of the Israeli Mossad intelligence organization (Bund. James Bund!).

Question #85: What Israeli religious group reveres Jethro, Moses' father-in-law?

א: The Bedouins.

ב: The Clampetts.

ג: The Bahais.

ד: The Druse.

ה: Beit Tull.

☆ ☆ ☆ ☆ ☆ ☆ ☆ ☆ ☆ ☆ ☆ ☆ ☆ ☆ ☆ ☆ ☆

Question #86: What do Hermann Cohen, Alfred M. Cohen, Gerson B. Cohen, and Henry Cohen have in common?

א: All are Orthodox rabbis in New York City.

ב: These are the real names of the Brothers Karamazov.

ג: All have served in the United States House of Representatives.

ד: They were the family members in the *Saturday Night Live* skit, "The Cohenheads."

ה: All have the last name of Cohen.

☆ ☆ ☆ ☆ ☆ ☆ ☆ ☆ ☆ ☆ ☆ ☆ ☆ ☆ ☆ ☆ ☆

Question #87: Why is Purim called the Feast of Lots?

א: Because you are supposed to drink lots of alcohol and wear lots of make-up.

ב: Because gallows were set up for the hanging of the Jews on lots across from Ahashverus' palace.

ג: Lots is the Yiddish word for pastries, referring to hamantashen.

ד: Because Haman drew lots to determine the date upon which the Jews would be hanged.

ה: Because G-d spared Lot's life on Purim, when he destroyed Sodom and Gomorrah.

Question #88: What did Roy Millenson bury at the South Pole?

א: An electronic targeting device for secret experiments carried out by Israel's Air Force.

ב: His tefillin, which had worn out.

ג: A matzah ball. He was conducting experiments on freeze drying kosher foods for mail order overnight shipments.

ד: A fork, which he had unkoshered when stabbing a crazed penguin.

ה: A co-worker who died while they worked together at the South Pole Observatory, as Jewish law required a burial within 24 hours.

✧ ✧ ✧ ✧ ✧ ✧ ✧ ✧ ✧ ✧ ✧ ✧ ✧ ✧ ✧ ✧ ✧ ✧ ✧

Question #89: What is Aaron Chwat's stage name?

א: Vanna White.

ב: Aaron Brown.

ג: Red Buttons.

ד: Blu Greenberg.

ה: Mr. Green Jeans.

✧ ✧ ✧ ✧ ✧ ✧ ✧ ✧ ✧ ✧ ✧ ✧ ✧ ✧ ✧ ✧ ✧ ✧ ✧

Question #90: In the Apocrypha, what is the story of Susanna about?

א: She cried over her lover who froze to death in the hot sun.

ב: She was falsely accused of adultery, but was vindicated.

ג: She was the first female prophetess of the Israelites.

ד: She came to pray at the Temple, but the elders turned her away because women were not allowed to do so.

ה: A concubine of King David, she was exiled by Batsheva.

Answers: #85 - ד   #86 - ה   #87 - ד

Question #91: In what valley is Absalom's Pillar located?

א: The Kidron Valley.

ב: The Jordan Valley.

ג: The Jezreel Valley.

ד: The Rudy Valley.

ה: Valley Chai.

Question #92: For what is Emanuel Celler known?

א: It is the storage facility for Manischewitz Kosher Wine in New York.

ב: He was the first Jewish member of the British House of Lords.

ג: He was the second Jew to serve on the United States Supreme Court.

ד: He founded Temple Emanuel in New York City.

ה: He served in the United States House of Representatives from New York for fifty years.

Question #93: What is Kohelet?

א: The smaller eastern wall of the Temple.

ב: A female kohen.

ג: The covering on a Torah scroll.

ד: The book of *Ecclesiastes*.

ה: A person who performs female circumcisions.

Answers: #88 - ב   #89 - ג   #90 - ב

Question #94: What do Emanuel Goldblatt, Moe Goldman, Jackie Goldsmith, and Don Goldstein have in common?

א: All were All-America college basketball players.

ב: They all won gold medals at the Summer Olympics, representing South Africa.

** c**: All belong to the law firm which represents the NFL Players Association.

ד: They were the Yeshiva University 1980 football team front four, known as "The Big Gold Guys."

ה: They were producers of the movie, *Goldfinger*.

✧ ✧ ✧ ✧ ✧ ✧ ✧ ✧ ✧ ✧ ✧ ✧ ✧ ✧ ✧ ✧ ✧ ✧ ✧

Question #95: Who was Jedediah?

א: One of Joseph's brothers.

ב: The leader of the biblical tribe, the Clampetts.

c: The wife of King Ammon of Judea.

ד: The priest who succeeded Aaron upon his death.

ה: A bullfrog mentioned in the story of the ten plagues.

✧ ✧ ✧ ✧ ✧ ✧ ✧ ✧ ✧ ✧ ✧ ✧ ✧ ✧ ✧ ✧ ✧ ✧ ✧

Question #96: What is Viddui?

א: The ceremony on Yom Kippur when the priests ascend the bimah.

ב: The Hebrew term for confession of sins.

c: Yiddish for "I saw," from the phrase "venui, viddui, vincui" – "I came, I saw, I conquered."

ד: The Hebrew term, derived from English, for video camera.

ה: Refers to Yom Viddui, "The Day of Why Do We?" when any Jew can approach the Grand Rebbe for an explanation of a Jewish law.

Answers: #91 - **א**   #92 - **ה**   #93 - **ד**

Question #97: For what was Emma Goldman arrested on March 27, 1915?

ℵ: She participated in a rally calling for the overthrow of the American government.

ℶ: She chained herself to the White House fence to protest American policy regarding Russia.

ℷ: She was found to be a card carrying Communist on a Saturday, in violation of the restrictions against carrying on Shabbat.

ℸ: She was caught shoplifting from Saks Fifth Avenue.

ה: She delivered the first public speech in the United States on the use of contraceptives.

✧ ✧ ✧ ✧ ✧ ✧ ✧ ✧ ✧ ✧ ✧ ✧ ✧ ✧ ✧ ✧ ✧ ✧ ✧

Question #98: Who was the Russian world champion chess master who lost his title to Bobby Fischer in 1972?

ℵ: Boris Yeltsin.

ℶ: Boris Becker.

ℷ: Victor Petrenko.

ℸ: Boris Badenov.

ה: Boris Spassky.

✧ ✧ ✧ ✧ ✧ ✧ ✧ ✧ ✧ ✧ ✧ ✧ ✧ ✧ ✧ ✧ ✧ ✧ ✧

Question #99: What is Cheshvan?

ℵ: An Israeli vehicle which holds seven passengers.

ℶ: The first kibbutz, established in 1909.

ℷ: The second month of the year in the Jewish calendar.

ℸ: The seven day mourning period.

ה: A flat bread traditionally served by Sephardic Jews on Shabbat, rather than Challah.

Answers: #94 - ℵ   #95 - ℷ   #96 - ℶ

Question #100: Who was Gaspar da Gama?

א: He was a Jewish navigator who was pressed into service by the Portuguese explorer Vasco da Gama, whose name he took when he underwent a forced Baptism.

ב: He was a Portuguese navigator who opened the sea route to the Cape of Good Hope.

ג: This is the Sephardic name of Caspar the Friendly Ghost.

ד: He was the prime minister of Spain who ended the Inquisition.

ה: He was a disciple of Maimonides in Spain in the 12th century.

✡ ✡ ✡ ✡ ✡ ✡ ✡ ✡ ✡ ✡ ✡ ✡ ✡ ✡ ✡ ✡ ✡

Question #101: What is Emunah?

א: One of the notes of the shofar.

ב: Refers to the high priest in the Temple.

ג: A heavenly body, as in "when emunah hits your eye like a big pizza pie."

ד: Faith.

ה: Repentance.

✡ ✡ ✡ ✡ ✡ ✡ ✡ ✡ ✡ ✡ ✡ ✡ ✡ ✡ ✡ ✡ ✡

Question #102: Of the twelve tribes, which two were not named after sons of Jacob?

א: Dan and Naphtali.

ב: Zebulun and Issachar.

ג: Ephraim and Manasseh.

ד: Sioux and Iroquois.

ה: Asher and Levi.

Answers: #97 - **ה**   #98 - **ה**   #99 - **ג**

Question #103: What did Doron Menashe of Israel do 22,200 times in three hours?

ℵ: Pick Jaffa oranges.

ℶ: Bounce a soccer ball on his foot.

ℷ: Recite the Sh'ma.

ℸ: Belch, after eating too many felafels.

ℎ: Bounce on a trampoline.

☆ ☆ ☆ ☆ ☆ ☆ ☆ ☆ ☆ ☆ ☆ ☆ ☆ ☆ ☆ ☆ ☆

Question #104: What was Auto-emancipation?

ℵ: A pamphlet by Judah Loeb Pinsker in 1882 which called for the establishment of a Jewish state so Jews could save themselves from anti-semitism.

ℶ: The proclamation in 1834 by Queen Isabella II of Spain which ended the Inquisition and allowed Jews to return to Spain.

ℷ: The law which forbids the driving of cars in religious neighborhoods in Israel on the Shabbat and holidays.

ℸ: The religious ceremony wherein Jews living under slavery can become symbolically free through repentance to G-d.

ℎ: The law which ended the ban on importation of German cars to Israel.

☆ ☆ ☆ ☆ ☆ ☆ ☆ ☆ ☆ ☆ ☆ ☆ ☆ ☆ ☆ ☆ ☆

Question #105: Jascha Heifetz is renowned for playing what instrument?

ℵ: Viola.

ℶ: Piano.

ℷ: Violin.

ℸ: Jews harp.

ℎ: Shofar.

Answers: #100 - ℵ   #101 - ℸ   #102 - ℷ

Question #106: What is Derech Eretz?

א: The name of the major atlas of Israeli roads.

ב: A nickname for Israel, the "Proper Homeland" of the Jewish people.

ג: The title given by Sephardim to the chief rabbi of the community.

ד: This refers to proper behavior and respect between people.

ה: Derek Jeter's real name.

☆ ☆ ☆ ☆ ☆ ☆ ☆ ☆ ☆ ☆ ☆ ☆ ☆ ☆ ☆ ☆ ☆ ☆

Question #107: To what did Golda Meyerson change her name?

א: Goldie Hawn.

ב: Golda Meir.

ג: Bess Myerson.

ד: Metro-Goldwyn-Mayer.

ה: Elle McPherson.

☆ ☆ ☆ ☆ ☆ ☆ ☆ ☆ ☆ ☆ ☆ ☆ ☆ ☆ ☆ ☆ ☆ ☆

Question #108: What is the Choshen?

א: The period of time between the shiva period and the end of the year of mourning.

ב: The breastplate placed over the Torah scroll.

ג: A book by Chaim Potok, about a drunken yeshiva bocher.

ד: This is the name of the straps on the tefillin.

ה: The person who reads the Torah in the Yemenite Jewish community.

Question #109: For what was Reuben Ticker known?

א: He was a famous opera star, better known as Richard Tucker.

ב: He invented the ticker tape used by the stock market.

ג: He was the first president of Hebrew Union College.

ד: He won the Nobel prize for his work in economics at Harvard.

ה: He invented the artificial heart.

✡ ✡ ✡ ✡ ✡ ✡ ✡ ✡ ✡ ✡ ✡ ✡ ✡ ✡ ✡ ✡ ✡ ✡

Question #110: What is Goldeneh Medinah?

א: Golden Mountain, the name given to Jerusalem by immigrants from Europe in the early 1900's.

ב: Land of Gold, a reference to the United States, which was seen by European Jews as a place where the streets were paved with gold.

ג: Golda Meir's real name.

ד: The Yiddish name for the Golden Calf.

ה: A type of goldfish caught in the Mediterranean sea, it is used in Israeli gefilte fish.

✡ ✡ ✡ ✡ ✡ ✡ ✡ ✡ ✡ ✡ ✡ ✡ ✡ ✡ ✡ ✡ ✡

Question #111: What is it called when Jews symbolically cast out their sins on the water?

א: Sin shpritzing.

ב: Tishri.

ג: Tashlich.

ד: Geshem.

ה: Mishloach manot.

Answers: #106 - **ד**   *#107 -* **ב**   *#108 -* **ב**

Question #112: What performer was discovered by Eddie Cantor and became a famous movie star?

א: Shirley Temple Black.

ב: Joel Grey.

ג: Pinky Lee.

ד: Al Green.

ה: Red Rover.

✧ ✧ ✧ ✧ ✧ ✧ ✧ ✧ ✧ ✧ ✧ ✧ ✧ ✧ ✧ ✧ ✧ ✧

Question #113: What is Shucklin?

א: The traditional method of chanting the Torah.

ב: The swaying motion, typical of traditional Jews when praying.

ג: The ceremonial peeling of outer leaves from ears of corn.

ד: A Yemenite dance.

ה: Going shopping in the Arab markets.

✧ ✧ ✧ ✧ ✧ ✧ ✧ ✧ ✧ ✧ ✧ ✧ ✧ ✧ ✧ ✧ ✧ ✧

Question #114: Who was Hagar?

א: Founder of the company which makes Hagar slacks.

ב: A Viking leader who stormed Jerusalem in the sixth century.

ג: The Egyptian maidservant of Sarah, who became a concubine to Abraham and gave birth to Ishmael.

ד: A minor prophet who foretold the destruction of the Second Temple.

ה: She was the mother of Moses.

Question #115: For what is Francis Salvador known?

ה: He was the first Jew killed in the American revolution.

ב: To escape the Inquisition, he sailed with Columbus, and was responsible for the founding of El Salvador.

ג: This is the real name of the Sephardic Jew who later became known as Frank Sinatra.

ד: He was the first Jew to serve in the United States Senate.

ה: He was the Boston Strangler.

✿ ✿ ✿ ✿ ✿ ✿ ✿ ✿ ✿ ✿ ✿ ✿ ✿ ✿ ✿ ✿ ✿ ✿

Question #116: What two cities were destroyed by G-d because of the sins of their inhabitants?

ה: Shiloh and Gedera.

ב: Pithom and Raamses.

ג: Simon and Garfunkel.

ד: Sodom and Gomorrah.

ה: Jerusalem and Jericho.

✿ ✿ ✿ ✿ ✿ ✿ ✿ ✿ ✿ ✿ ✿ ✿ ✿ ✿ ✿ ✿ ✿ ✿

Question #117: What philanthropist provided funds for Israel's first commercial vineyard?

ה: Edgar Bronfman.

ב: James Rothschild.

ג: Manny Shevitz.

ד: Ernest Gallo.

ה: Doug and Wendy Winer.

Answers: #112 - ב   #113 - ב   #114 - ג

Question #118: What is Chanukat Habayit?

א: The dedication of a new home.

ב: The celebration of Chanukah in the home.

ג: The name of the original celebration of Chanukah by the Maccabees.

ד: The traditional request by children to their parents to "buy it for Chanukah."

ה: A lesser known holiday celebrating the miraculous burning of a light bulb outside the Lubavitcher Rebbe's house for eight years.

✡ ✡ ✡ ✡ ✡ ✡ ✡ ✡ ✡ ✡ ✡ ✡ ✡ ✡ ✡ ✡ ✡ ✡

Question #119: What was the professional name of composer Israel Baline?

א: Irving Berlin.

ב: Isaac Bashevis Singer.

ג: Ice Cube.

ד: Ira Gershwin.

ה: Beth Israel.

✡ ✡ ✡ ✡ ✡ ✡ ✡ ✡ ✡ ✡ ✡ ✡ ✡ ✡ ✡ ✡ ✡ ✡

Question #120: What is Khazaria?

א: The land east of Canaan from which the Khazarites attacked the Israelites.

ב: A Jewish state that existed in Crimea from the 7th to the 10th centuries.

ג: Refers to the biblical list of unkosher animals.

ד: A city on the Israeli coast which features an ancient Roman amphitheater.

ה: A stomach virus suffered by Jews who eat pork.

Question #121: What nationality was Delilah?

א: Amorite.

ב: Jebusite.

ג: Philistine.

ד: Hittite.

ה: Samsonite.

✧ ✧ ✧ ✧ ✧ ✧ ✧ ✧ ✧ ✧ ✧ ✧ ✧ ✧ ✧ ✧ ✧ ✧

Question #122: What song did the Jews sing while crossing the Red Sea?

א: Let My People Go.

ב: Splish Splash.

ג: Adon Olam.

ד: Oseh Shalom.

ה: Az Yashir.

✧ ✧ ✧ ✧ ✧ ✧ ✧ ✧ ✧ ✧ ✧ ✧ ✧ ✧ ✧ ✧ ✧ ✧

Question #123: Who was Judah Solomon Chai Alkalai?

א: A 20th century rabbinic orator known for his acidic tongue.

ב: This is the real name of Haym Salomon, the financier who financed the American revolution.

ג: A leader of the National Religious Party in Israel.

ד: A rabbi of the 19th century who was an early proponent of Zionism.

ה: He invented the recipe for Chai tea.

Question #124: What is Maimonides' eighth (lowest) level of charity?

א: Giving after the poor person asks.

ב: Giving willingly, but only to rich people.

ג: Giving, but not giving as much as one can afford.

ד: Giving begrudgingly.

ה: Giving day old bagels.

☆ ☆ ☆ ☆ ☆ ☆ ☆ ☆ ☆ ☆ ☆ ☆ ☆ ☆ ☆ ☆ ☆ ☆

Question #125: What was the stage name of Frederick Austerlitz?

א: Fred McMurray.

ב: Fred Astaire.

ג: Fred Flintstone.

ד: Fred Durst.

ה: Freddy Kruger.

☆ ☆ ☆ ☆ ☆ ☆ ☆ ☆ ☆ ☆ ☆ ☆ ☆ ☆ ☆ ☆ ☆ ☆

Question #126: Who was Isaac Bernays?

א: A German rabbi of the 19th century, he was the first Orthodox rabbi to preach in German.

ב: He founded the Satmar sect of Chassidim.

ג: He was the first president of the Jewish Theological Seminary.

ד: This was a pen name used by Isaac Bashevis Singer.

ה: He invented a kosher cooking sauce.

Answers: #121 - ג   *#122 -* ה   *#123 -* ד

Question #127: What were the names of Rebecca's twin sons?

א: David and Jonathan.

ב: Jacob and Esau.

ג: Ham and Shem.

ד: Ham and Eggs.

ה: Tiki and Rondé.

✿ ✿ ✿ ✿ ✿ ✿ ✿ ✿ ✿ ✿ ✿ ✿ ✿ ✿ ✿ ✿ ✿ ✿

Question #128: What popular bar mitzvah party song has been recorded by Miriam Makeba, Sergio Franchi, Eartha Kitt, Connie Francis, and Harry Belafonte?

א: Sunrise Sunset.

ב: Hevenu Shalom Aleichem.

ג: Hava Nagilah.

ד: Hot Hot Hot.

ה: Zum Golly Golly.

✿ ✿ ✿ ✿ ✿ ✿ ✿ ✿ ✿ ✿ ✿ ✿ ✿ ✿ ✿ ✿ ✿

Question #129: What is the Bintel Brief?

א: An argument filed by Alan Dershowitz on behalf of a Jewish prisoner who demanded the availability of kosher food in prison; the Supreme Court ruled in favor and established this right for Jewish prisoners.

ב: The legal document, issued in 1967 by Chaim Bintel, the head of the Israeli Supreme Court, which declared that Jerusalem is the capital of Israel.

ג: The blanket in which an infant boy is swaddled prior to the circumcision ceremony.

ד: Underwear worn by Chassidic men in Poland.

ה: An advice column in the Yiddish newspaper, the *Forward*.

Answers: #124 - ד   #125 - ב   #126 - א

Question #130: What is G'lilah?

א: The wife of Samson.

ב: The procession around the sanctuary with the Torah scroll before and after the Torah reading.

ג: Refers to the traditional Chassidic song fest held on the birthday of the Rebbe.

ד: The honor of dressing the Torah after it has been read.

ה: The honor of dressing the Rabbi after he reads Torah.

✡ ✡ ✡ ✡ ✡ ✡ ✡ ✡ ✡ ✡ ✡ ✡ ✡ ✡ ✡ ✡ ✡

Question #131: What were the names of Tevye's daughters in "Fiddler On The Roof"?

א: Tzeitel, Hodel, Chava, Shayna, and Chanala.

ב: Tzeitel, Hodel, Chava, Shprintze, and Beilke.

ג: Tzeitel, Hodel, Chava, Fyedka, and Motel.

ד: Jennifer, Ashley, Tiphanie, Jessica, and Danielle.

ה: Phoebe, Monica, Rachel, Chandler, and Ross.

✡ ✡ ✡ ✡ ✡ ✡ ✡ ✡ ✡ ✡ ✡ ✡ ✡ ✡ ✡ ✡ ✡

Question #132: What is Lamdan?

א: A Talmudic scholar, usually a layman.

ב: The ceremonial sacrifice of a sheep at the Temple in Jerusalem.

ג: The Islamic month where daytime fasting is required.

ד: The person who washes and dresses the deceased before a funeral.

ה: When Joseph was sold into slavery by his brothers, he looked at his brother Dan and said, "Lama, Dan?" ("Why, Dan?"). A lamdan now refers to anyone who betrays a friend or relative.

Question #133: What is Judezmo?

א: Meaning "Jewish month" in Italian, this is the name of the monthly Rosh Chodesh celebration in the Roman Jewish community.

ב: The name which Sephardic Jews use to refer to Judea and Samaria.

ג: A Jewish language, related to Ladino.

ד: The Hebrew version of *Hey Jude*.

ה: The Jewish museum in Prague.

✿ ✿ ✿ ✿ ✿ ✿ ✿ ✿ ✿ ✿ ✿ ✿ ✿ ✿ ✿ ✿

Question #134: What is the connection between Golda Meir and Pocahontas?

א: Both were the first female leaders of their people.

ב: Golda Meir was known in Milwaukee for her portrayal of Pocahontas in her elementary school Thanksgiving play.

ג: Pocahontas translates as "golden light," as does Golda Meir.

ד: Pocahontas was the name of the ship upon which Golda Meir sailed to Israel in 1921.

ה: In a poll given to Jewish Indians, they came in first and second place to the question "Name your favorite women in history."

✿ ✿ ✿ ✿ ✿ ✿ ✿ ✿ ✿ ✿ ✿ ✿ ✿ ✿ ✿ ✿

Question #135: What was Moses' mother's name?

א: Yocheved.

ב: Miriam.

ג: Grandma Moses.

ד: Esther.

ה: Chana.

Answers: #130 - ד   #131 - ב   #132 - א

Question #136: What celebrity first became famous for answering questions about boxing on "The $64,000 Question"?

א: Howard Cosell.

ב: Bob Arum.

ג: Joyce Brothers.

ד: Cassius Clay.

ה: Slappy White.

✧ ✧ ✧ ✧ ✧ ✧ ✧ ✧ ✧ ✧ ✧ ✧ ✧ ✧ ✧ ✧ ✧ ✧

Question #137: Who was responsible for the abolition of corporal punishment in the United States Navy?

א: Commodore Uriah P. Levy.

ב: Admiral Hyman Rickover.

ג: Rabbi Isaac Mayer Wise.

ד: Rear Admiral Abraham Potchtush.

ה: Major General Frederick Knefler.

✧ ✧ ✧ ✧ ✧ ✧ ✧ ✧ ✧ ✧ ✧ ✧ ✧ ✧ ✧ ✧ ✧ ✧

Question #138: Who was Primo Levi?

א: Refers to Jacob's son Levi, who was the first Levite.

ב: The first Jewish prime minister of Italy.

ג: An Italian author who wrote about the Holocaust.

ד: Father of Dolly Levi, of *Hello Dolly* fame.

ה: A rock band in Israel whose members are all Levites.

Question #139: Who was Lina Morenstern?

ℵ: Rhoda Morgenstern's mother.

ℶ: This is Leonard Nimoy's real name.

ℷ: She was the founder of ORT.

ℸ: She was the director of such movies as *Swept Away* and *Seven Beauties*.

ℇ: She established Berlin's first free food kitchen, and convened the first International Women's Congress.

✡ ✡ ✡ ✡ ✡ ✡ ✡ ✡ ✡ ✡ ✡ ✡ ✡ ✡ ✡ ✡ ✡ ✡

Question #140: Who was the first Conservative woman rabbi?

ℵ: Amy Irving.

ℶ: Amy Eilberg.

ℷ: Amy Fisher.

ℸ: Amy Goldstein.

ℇ: Rabbi Shankar.

✡ ✡ ✡ ✡ ✡ ✡ ✡ ✡ ✡ ✡ ✡ ✡ ✡ ✡ ✡ ✡ ✡ ✡

Question #141: This duo's first hit was "The Sound Of Silence."

ℵ: Simon and Schuster.

ℶ: Oscar and Hammerstein.

ℷ: Lenny and Squiggy.

ℸ: Marcel Marceau and Harpo Marx.

ℇ: Simon and Garfunkel.

Question #142: What is the Yom Kippur Effect?

א: Refers to the phenomenon in New York wherein restaurants suffer their worst business day of the year on Erev Yom Kippur.

ב: Refers to a mood of sadness which overcomes Israelis on the anniversary of the Yom Kippur war.

ג: A finding by doctors in Chicago in a 1983 study that women who fast near the end of their pregnancy may go into early labor.

ד: This refers to a meditative state which the truly repentant enter, wherein they believe that G-d stands by their side.

ה: Refers to the feeling of sorrow and repentance which sets in upon hearing the chanting of the Kol Nidre prayer by the cantor.

✡ ✡ ✡ ✡ ✡ ✡ ✡ ✡ ✡ ✡ ✡ ✡ ✡ ✡ ✡ ✡ ✡ ✡

Question #143: What performer was associated with the song "Hooray For Captain Spaulding"?

א: Sammy Davis, Jr.

ב: Captain Kangaroo.

ג: Groucho Marx.

ד: Abner Doubleday.

ה: Captain & Tenille.

✡ ✡ ✡ ✡ ✡ ✡ ✡ ✡ ✡ ✡ ✡ ✡ ✡ ✡ ✡ ✡ ✡ ✡

Question #144: Which wild west figure was married to Josephine Sarah Marcus?

א: Bat Masterson.

ב: Jesse James.

ג: Wyatt Earp.

ד: John Wayne.

ה: Avram Belinsky.

Answers: #139 - ה   #140 - ב   #141 - ה

Question #145: Who was Hezekiah?

ה: A king of Judea.

ב: The second wife of Samson.

ג: A Palestinian terrorist group.

ד: The high priest at the Second Temple at the time of its destruction.

ה: A bullfrog mentioned in the story of the ten plagues.

✧ ✧ ✧ ✧ ✧ ✧ ✧ ✧ ✧ ✧ ✧ ✧ ✧ ✧ ✧ ✧ ✧

Question #146: Who wrote "Fear Of Flying"?

ה: Avi O. Fobick.

ב: Neil Armstrong.

ג: Louis Nizer.

ד: Joseph Heller.

ה: Erica Jong.

✧ ✧ ✧ ✧ ✧ ✧ ✧ ✧ ✧ ✧ ✧ ✧ ✧ ✧ ✧ ✧ ✧

Question #147: Who left the Supreme Court amid charges of financial irregularities?

ה: Arthur Goldberg.

ב: Abe Fortas.

ג: Benjamin Cardozo.

ד: Diana Ross.

ה: Andrew Fastow.

Answers: #142 - ג   #143 - ג   #144 - ג

Question #148: Who was Philo of Alexandria?

א: A commentator in Egypt who wrote on metaphysics, ethics, and Bible commentary.

ב: An Egyptian minister who advised the Pharaoh not to free the Israelites.

ג: He was the Pharaoh whose dreams Joseph interpreted while in Egypt.

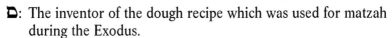

ד: The inventor of the dough recipe which was used for matzah during the Exodus.

ה: The author of the manuscripts found in the Cairo Genizah.

✡ ✡ ✡ ✡ ✡ ✡ ✡ ✡ ✡ ✡ ✡ ✡ ✡ ✡ ✡ ✡ ✡ ✡ ✡

Question #149: Which was not a real TV show with Jewish characters & themes?

א: Lanigan's Rabbi.

ב: Brooklyn Bridge.

ג: Saturday Night at the Matzah Ball.

ד: Menasha the Magnificent.

ה: The Gertrude Berg Show.

✡ ✡ ✡ ✡ ✡ ✡ ✡ ✡ ✡ ✡ ✡ ✡ ✡ ✡ ✡ ✡ ✡ ✡ ✡

Question #150: Who actually committed the treason for which Captain Dreyfus was arrested and jailed?

א: Georges Clemenceau.

ב: Emile Zola.

ג: Benedict Arnold.

ד: Inspector Jacques Clouseau.

ה: Major Marie Charles Esterhazy.

Question #151: Who are Ham, Shem, and Japeth?

ℵ: Haman's three courtiers.

ℶ: Noah's three sons.

ℷ: The Three Stooges.

ℸ: The Three Little Pigs.

ℶ: The Three Wise Men.

✡ ✡ ✡ ✡ ✡ ✡ ✡ ✡ ✡ ✡ ✡ ✡ ✡ ✡ ✡ ✡ ✡

Question #152: Who was Solomon ben Simeon Duran?

ℵ: A rabbinical authority of the 1400's, known as the Rashbash.

ℶ: A disciple of Hillel, who became head of Beit Hillel after Hillel's death.

ℷ: The first chief rabbi of Israel, appointed in 1948 by ben-Gurion.

ℸ: Founder of the rock group Duran Duran.

ℶ: He was one of the authors of the Dead Sea Scrolls.

✡ ✡ ✡ ✡ ✡ ✡ ✡ ✡ ✡ ✡ ✡ ✡ ✡ ✡ ✡ ✡ ✡

Question #153: Why will Ed Ames be remembered for wielding a tomahawk?

ℵ: He performed a bris using this unconventional tool.

ℶ: He launched a tomahawk missile in a promotional film for the Israeli army.

ℷ: He was the first to do the Tomahawk Chop at an Atlanta Braves game. After a few unfortunate accidents, stadium officials banned use of real tomahawks, and now the action is performed with foam rubber tomahawks.

ℸ: He threw it at a target on the *Tonight Show starring Johnny Carson*, hitting the target below the belt.

ℶ: He used it on a cow in a training film for kosher butchers.

Answers: #148 - ℵ   #149 - ℷ   #150 - ℶ

Question #154: Who created Superman?

ﬡ: Stan Lee and Jack Kirby.

ﬡ: Richard Donner.

ﬡ: Jerry Siegel and Joe Schuster.

ﬡ: Jor-el and Lara.

ﬡ: Ma and Pa Kent.

☆ ☆ ☆ ☆ ☆ ☆ ☆ ☆ ☆ ☆ ☆ ☆ ☆ ☆ ☆ ☆ ☆

Question #155: Who are the seven guests we traditionally invite to be with us in the Sukkah?

ﬡ: Abraham, Isaac, Jacob, Sarah, Rebecca, Rachel, and Leah.

ﬡ: Abraham, Isaac, Jacob, Joseph, Moses, Aaron, and David.

ﬡ: Abraham, Isaac, Jacob, Noah, Moses, Solomon, and David.

ﬡ: Abraham, Martin, John, Groucho, Harpo, Chico, and Zeppo.

ﬡ: The rabbi, the cantor, the synagogue president, the religious school principal, the synagogue administrator, the nursery school director, and the custodian.

☆ ☆ ☆ ☆ ☆ ☆ ☆ ☆ ☆ ☆ ☆ ☆ ☆ ☆ ☆ ☆ ☆

Question #156: What was the Zion Mule Corps?

ﬡ: A Jewish military organization founded by Joseph Trumpeldor.

ﬡ: Founded in 1895, it was the first public transportation company in Palestine.

ﬡ: A kosher meat company in Israel.

ﬡ: The drug smuggling division of the Israeli Mafia.

ﬡ: An organization of stubbornly pro-Israeli American Jews.

Answers: *#151 - ﬡ*   *#152 - ﬡ*   *#153 - ﬡ*

Question #157: Who was the first Jewish chaplain in the United States Army?

א: Isaac Mayer Wise.

ב: Charlie Chaplain.

ג: Yitzhak Mulcahey.

ד: Judah Magnes.

ה: Jacob Frankel.

✧ ✧ ✧ ✧ ✧ ✧ ✧ ✧ ✧ ✧ ✧ ✧ ✧ ✧ ✧ ✧ ✧ ✧

Question #158: What is the meaning of the term Amora?

א: Love, as in "when the moon hits your eye like a big pizza pie, that's amora."

ב: Refers to Talmudic sages in the 3rd through 6th centuries.

ג: Refers to a teacher.

ד: Refers to the oral law.

ה: It is an Israeli designed tank.

✧ ✧ ✧ ✧ ✧ ✧ ✧ ✧ ✧ ✧ ✧ ✧ ✧ ✧ ✧ ✧ ✧ ✧

Question #159: Who was the first high commissioner to Palestine, during the British mandate?

א: Dag Hammarskjold.

ב: Benjamin Disraeli.

ג: Lloyd George.

ד: Timothy Leary.

ה: Herbert Samuel.

Answers: #154 - ג   #155 - ב   #156 - א

Question #160: Who was the first president of the American Federation of Labor?

א: Samuel Goldwyn.

ב: Samuel Gompers.

ג: David Dubinsky.

ד: Dr. Spock.

ה: Eugene V. Debs.

✿ ✿ ✿ ✿ ✿ ✿ ✿ ✿ ✿ ✿ ✿ ✿ ✿ ✿ ✿ ✿ ✿ ✿ ✿

Question #161: Which of the following is not one of the 613 commandments?

א: A man who unjustly accuses his wife of infidelity must divorce her.

ב: Cattle to be sacrificed must be at least eight days old.

ג: A person with leprosy must shave off all of his hair.

ד: You must examine locusts to determine whether they may be eaten.

ה: A eunuch may not marry a Jewess.

✿ ✿ ✿ ✿ ✿ ✿ ✿ ✿ ✿ ✿ ✿ ✿ ✿ ✿ ✿ ✿ ✿ ✿ ✿

Question #162: Who wrote "My Michael" and "Perfect Peace In The Land Of Israel"?

א: Amos Mansdorf.

ב: Amos Oz.

ג: Amos Elon.

ד: Amos & Andy.

ה: Tori Amos.

Question #163: Which statement is false?

א: A star of TV's *Mission Impossible* always wore his yarmulke under a toupee while performing.

ב: Fidel Castro is of Jewish descent. His family emigrated to Cuba during the Inquisition.

ג: Rashad A-Shawa, a grandson of a mayor of Gaza, is Jewish.

ד: The only man who survived the battle of the Alamo was Jewish.

ה: Gene Simmons, of Kiss, once studied to be a rabbi.

✡ ✡ ✡ ✡ ✡ ✡ ✡ ✡ ✡ ✡ ✡ ✡ ✡ ✡ ✡ ✡ ✡ ✡

Question #164: Who created the voices of Bugs Bunny, Daffy Duck, and Porky Pig?

א: Mel Blanc.

ב: Mel Brooks.

ג: Mel Allen.

ד: Larry "Bud" Melman.

ה: Melanie Griffith.

✡ ✡ ✡ ✡ ✡ ✡ ✡ ✡ ✡ ✡ ✡ ✡ ✡ ✡ ✡ ✡ ✡ ✡

Question #165: Why was Ahad Ha'am famous in Jewish history?

א: He was Judah Maccabee's first lieutenant.

ב: He is the only Israeli to ever win the Pulitzer Prize for poetry.

ג: He was president of the first Knesset in Israel.

ד: He was the father of "spiritual Zionism."

ה: He changed his name from I'had Ham, to make a statement about kashrut.

Answers: #160 - ב   #161 - א   #162 - ב

Question #166: Who were the Frankists?

א: An organization dedicated to the memory of Anne Frank.

ב: Followers of the false messiah, Jacob Frank.

ג: A small Jewish sect who only eat Hebrew National hot dogs.

ד: A sect of Jews who believe in the burning of incense during the Torah reading, to increase the sweetness of the experience.

ה: A group of Israelis who believed that Jews should not have to pay postage to mail letters from Israel.

✡ ✡ ✡ ✡ ✡ ✡ ✡ ✡ ✡ ✡ ✡ ✡ ✡ ✡ ✡ ✡ ✡ ✡

Question #167: Which of the following are not nicknames for great rabbinic scholars?

א: Rif, Rashi, and Rabbenu Tam.

ב: Rambam, Ramban, and Rema.

ג: Rabad, Raban, and Rabiah.

ד: Taz, Shakh, and Maharam.

ה: Raffi, Rottini, and Rugelach.

✡ ✡ ✡ ✡ ✡ ✡ ✡ ✡ ✡ ✡ ✡ ✡ ✡ ✡ ✡ ✡ ✡ ✡

Question #168: Who wrote "The Odd Couple"?

א: Maria Shriver and Arnold Schwarzenegger.

ב: Nora Ephron.

ג: Garry Marshall.

ד: Jack Klugman.

ה: Neil Simon.

Answers: #163 - ג   *#164 -* א   *#165 -* ד

Question #169: Who founded Reconstructionism?

א: Mordechai Kaplan.

ב: Stephen Wise.

ג: Tim Allen.

ד: Solomon Schechter.

ה: Bob the Builder.

✧ ✧ ✧ ✧ ✧ ✧ ✧ ✧ ✧ ✧ ✧ ✧ ✧ ✧ ✧ ✧ ✧ ✧

*Question #170: Who was the president of the International Ladies'
Garment Workers' Union from 1932-1966?*

א: Frederick Mellinger.

ב: Leonard Garment.

ג: David Dubinsky.

ד: John L. Lewis.

ה: Jimmy Hoffa.

✧ ✧ ✧ ✧ ✧ ✧ ✧ ✧ ✧ ✧ ✧ ✧ ✧ ✧ ✧ ✧ ✧ ✧

Question #171: To what does Atlit refer?

א: The first kibbutz founded in Israel.

ב: The cover of a Torah scroll.

ג: The Israeli kibbutz dairy cooperative.

ד: Israeli ruins located near Mt. Carmel.

ה: A member of the Israeli Olympic team.

Answers: *#166 -* ב   *#167 -* ה   *#168 -* ה

Question #172: When Jacob wrestled all night long to defeat another man, he was given a new name. What was it?

א: Hulk Hogan.

ב: Shechem.

ג: Ha-even.

ד: Chazak.

ה: Israel.

☆ ☆ ☆ ☆ ☆ ☆ ☆ ☆ ☆ ☆ ☆ ☆ ☆ ☆ ☆ ☆ ☆ ☆

Question #173: What Yiddish theater song was sung by such performers as Ella Fitzgerald and The Andrews Sisters?

א: Tum Balalaika.

ב: Bay Mir Bistu Sheyn.

ג: My Yiddishe Mamma.

ד: Ooo Eee Ooo Ah Ah, Ting Tang Walla Walla Bing Bang.

ה: Ikh Bin A Kleyner Dreydl.

☆ ☆ ☆ ☆ ☆ ☆ ☆ ☆ ☆ ☆ ☆ ☆ ☆ ☆ ☆ ☆ ☆ ☆

Question #174: Where is Theodore Herzl buried?

א: In Grant's tomb.

ב: In front of the Knesset building.

ג: On Mount Herzl.

ד: In Basle, Switzerland.

ה: In Herzliyah.

Answers: #169 - א   #170 - ג   #171 - ד

Question #175: What were the names of the storage cities built by Jewish slaves in Egypt?

א: Cairo and Suez.

ב: Pithom and Raamses.

ג: Raamses and Lewis.

ד: Alexandria and Ismailiya.

ה: Aswan and Luxor.

✿ ✿ ✿ ✿ ✿ ✿ ✿ ✿ ✿ ✿ ✿ ✿ ✿ ✿ ✿ ✿ ✿

Question #176: What is Tzitzit?

א: The ritual fringes on the corners of the tallit.

ב: A Mediterranean fly which can carry diseases.

ג: A Chassidic gathering where participants sit in a circle and share stories.

ד: The Israeli version of the *Sesame Street* character Big Bird.

ה: The Hebrew equivalent of the Yiddish "kumsitz," an informal gathering.

✿ ✿ ✿ ✿ ✿ ✿ ✿ ✿ ✿ ✿ ✿ ✿ ✿ ✿ ✿ ✿ ✿

Question #177: What is meant by the phrase "Bishop of the Jews"?

א: This refers to the leader of the Chassidic movement.

ב: A nickname for the Archbishop of New York, whose diocese includes the largest Jewish population in the world.

ג: This refers to Pope Benedict IV, who protected the Jews of Italy during the Inquisition.

ד: The term in medieval England for a kohen.

ה: This is what Dean Martin called Joey Bishop.

Answers: #172 - ה   *#173 -* ב   *#174 -* ג

Question #178: Which of the following English words come from Hebrew?

א: Apple, shoe, window.

ב: Pickle, hammer, mosaic.

ג: Ebony, asphalt, scallion.

ד: Moron, ninny, noodle.

ה: Yachts, cats, putts.

✡ ✡ ✡ ✡ ✡ ✡ ✡ ✡ ✡ ✡ ✡ ✡ ✡ ✡ ✡ ✡ ✡ ✡ ✡

Question #179: What is the Negev?

א: The tank which was instrumental in the Israeli march across the Sinai Desert in the Six Day War.

ב: The desert in the south of Israel.

ג: An anti-Zionist Chassidic sect, headed by the Negever Rebbe, formed in opposition to the pro-Zionist Positev Chassidim.

ד: The name of the superhighway between Tel Aviv and Jerusalem.

ה: The lake in the Galilee region of Israel.

✡ ✡ ✡ ✡ ✡ ✡ ✡ ✡ ✡ ✡ ✡ ✡ ✡ ✡ ✡ ✡ ✡ ✡

Question #180: Who wrote the book "Looking For Mr. Goodbar"?

א: Philip Roth.

ב: Milton Hershey.

ג: Saul Bellow.

ד: Nora Ephron.

ה: Judith Rossner.

Answers: *#175 -* ב   *#176 -* א   *#177 -* ד

Question #181: Who learned to blow the shofar at Congregation Herzl-Ner Tamid in Seattle?

🎵: Mr. T.

🎵: Sandra Dee.

🎵: Kenny G.

🎵: B. Dalton.

🎵: Louis Armstrong.

☆ ☆ ☆ ☆ ☆ ☆ ☆ ☆ ☆ ☆ ☆ ☆ ☆ ☆ ☆ ☆ ☆ ☆

Question #182: Where were the Dead Sea Scrolls found?

🎵: In King Tut's tomb.

🎵: Kuneitra.

🎵: Qumbaya.

🎵: Qumran.

🎵: In the Dead Sea.

☆ ☆ ☆ ☆ ☆ ☆ ☆ ☆ ☆ ☆ ☆ ☆ ☆ ☆ ☆ ☆ ☆ ☆

Question #183: Where did the name Chabad come from?

🎵: From the phrase, "the <u>ch</u>osen of <u>A</u>braham and <u>A</u>dam."

🎵: From the Hebrew words, "<u>ch</u>achma, <u>b</u>inah, <u>d</u>a'at," meaning wisdom, understanding, knowledge.

🎵: From the Hebrew, "<u>ch</u>am <u>b</u>a-bege<u>d</u>," meaning it's hot in these clothes, referring to the long black coats and hats worn by the Chassidim.

🎵: It is an abbreviation for "<u>Ch</u>assidic <u>b</u>a<u>d</u>ge," as the leaders in the Chabad movement wear their Chassidism as a badge of religious pride.

🎵: It's short for "<u>Ch</u>assids are real <u>b</u>ad <u>d</u>udes."

Answers: #178 - 🎵 *#179 -* 🎵 *#180 -* 🎵

Question #184: Who was Nehemiah?

ℵ: A governor of Judea who worked for social reforms.

ℶ: He was the only Israelite to oppose the creation of the golden calf when Moses went up Mt. Sinai to receive the Ten Commandments.

ℷ: The king of Israel who succeeded Solomon.

ℸ: He founded an Israeli grape drink company.

ℏ: A bullfrog mentioned in the story of the ten plagues.

✡ ✡ ✡ ✡ ✡ ✡ ✡ ✡ ✡ ✡ ✡ ✡ ✡ ✡ ✡ ✡ ✡ ✡

Question #185: Which of the following is not a real place in the United States named after a Jew?

ℵ: Brotmanville, NJ.

ℶ: Bunkie, LA.

ℷ: Spivak, CO.

ℸ: Strool, SD.

ℏ: Shmendrick, UT.

✡ ✡ ✡ ✡ ✡ ✡ ✡ ✡ ✡ ✡ ✡ ✡ ✡ ✡ ✡ ✡ ✡ ✡

Question #186: Who wrote the Psalms?

ℵ: King Psaul.

ℶ: King Solomon.

ℷ: King David.

ℸ: Joshua.

ℏ: Moses.

Answers: #181 - ℷ   #182 - ℸ   #183 - ℶ

Question #187: Who established the sperm oil industry in America?

א: Isaac Wesson.

ב: Jacob Rivera.

ג: Ron Jeremy.

ד: Judah Touro.

ה: Herman Melville.

☆ ☆ ☆ ☆ ☆ ☆ ☆ ☆ ☆ ☆ ☆ ☆ ☆ ☆ ☆ ☆ ☆

Question #188: Who founded the Chassidic movement?

א: Shmuley Boteach.

ב: Menachem Begin.

ג: Menachem Schneerson.

ד: Lar Lubovitch.

ה: The Ba'al Shem Tov.

☆ ☆ ☆ ☆ ☆ ☆ ☆ ☆ ☆ ☆ ☆ ☆ ☆ ☆ ☆ ☆ ☆

Question #189: What measured 440 feet x 73 feet x 44 feet?

א: The Western Wall in Jerusalem.

ב: Noah's ark.

ג: The largest matzah ball at the 1992 Haifa county fair.

ד: The ship "The Exodus."

ה: The pyramid built by Jewish slaves in Egypt.

Question #190: What did Ho Chi Minh offer to David ben-Gurion in 1946?

א: Migrant farm workers to assist with the kibbutz harvest.

ב: His mother's recipe for kosher Nuoc Cham (fish sauce).

ג: Weapons to use in fighting the Arabs.

ד: The first bagel franchise in Hanoi.

ה: Some land in Vietnam for a Jewish state.

✡ ✡ ✡ ✡ ✡ ✡ ✡ ✡ ✡ ✡ ✡ ✡ ✡ ✡ ✡ ✡ ✡

Question #191: For what was Zerubabel known?

א: He became governor of Israel when Jews were allowed to return there at the end of the Babylonian exile.

ב: He was the architect who built the Tower of Babel.

ג: He was the instigator of the creation of the golden calf at Mt. Sinai.

ד: It was the only kosher Laughing Cow cheese (Minibonbel and Minibabybel are not certified kosher).

ה: He was the king of Babylonia during the Babylonian exile.

✡ ✡ ✡ ✡ ✡ ✡ ✡ ✡ ✡ ✡ ✡ ✡ ✡ ✡ ✡ ✡ ✡

Question #192: What is Moriah?

א: The place where the Israelites first entered the Promised Land after crossing the desert.

ב: The spot where Abraham was ordered to offer Isaac in sacrifice to G-d.

ג: The strong dry winds which cross the Middle East.

ד: Cain's wife.

ה: The place where Moses died on the border of the Promised Land.

Answers: #187 - ב   #188 - ה   #189 - ב

Question #193: Who was the Jewish interpreter on Columbus's voyage to the New World?

ה: Cristóbal Colón.

ב: Juan Carlos de Toledo.

ג: Yosef Jiménez.

ד: Señor Wences.

ה: Luis de Torres.

✧ ✧ ✧ ✧ ✧ ✧ ✧ ✧ ✧ ✧ ✧ ✧ ✧ ✧ ✧ ✧ ✧ ✧

Question #194: What is the Triennial Cycle?

ה: A system of Torah reading which takes three years to complete, rather than one.

ב: The traditional gift given to a Chassidic boy on his third birthday, to celebrate his first hair cut.

ג: Refers to the reading of the Talmud, which takes three years to complete.

ד: Refers to a three part race in the Maccabean games, wherein cyclists must ride across the Negev, up and down Masada, and into the Dead Sea.

ה: Refers to a tradition among the Beta Yisrael (Ethiopian Jews) that women must go to the mikveh only three times a year.

✧ ✧ ✧ ✧ ✧ ✧ ✧ ✧ ✧ ✧ ✧ ✧ ✧ ✧ ✧ ✧ ✧

Question #195: Who emigrated to the United States from Poland at the age of 27 and founded a major cosmetics company?

ה: Estée Lauder.

ב: Max Factor.

ג: Helena Rubinstein.

ד: Avon Calling.

ה: Goldie Pimplepopper.

Question #196: Who founded the Henry Street Settlement in New York City?

א: Jane Addams.

ב: Henry Street.

ג: Lillian Wald.

ד: Rabbi Isaac Mayer Wise.

ה: Ed Koch.

✡ ✡ ✡ ✡ ✡ ✡ ✡ ✡ ✡ ✡ ✡ ✡ ✡ ✡ ✡ ✡ ✡ ✡ ✡

Question #197: What is the full name of the Israeli actor Topol?

א: Topol Feinshtein.

ב: Chaim Topol.

ג: Topol Gigio.

ד: Topol ben Moshe.

ה: Topol Toothpaste.

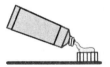

✡ ✡ ✡ ✡ ✡ ✡ ✡ ✡ ✡ ✡ ✡ ✡ ✡ ✡ ✡ ✡ ✡ ✡

Question #198: Which of the following was not a codifier of Jewish law?

א: Isaac ben Jacob ha-Lavan of Prague.

ב: Isaac ben Reuben of Duren.

ג: Isaac ben Moses of Vienna.

ד: Isaac ben Joseph of Corbeil.

ה: Isaac ben Hayes of Shaft.

Answers: #193 - ה   #194 - א   #195 - ב

Question #199: Which of the following are all kosher?

ה: Ibex, grasshopper, partridge.

ב: Llama, osprey, ant.

ג: Zebra, pelican, chameleon.

ד: Deer milk, gazelle milk, whale milk.

ה: Unicorn, jackalope, tribble.

☆ ☆ ☆ ☆ ☆ ☆ ☆ ☆ ☆ ☆ ☆ ☆ ☆ ☆ ☆ ☆ ☆ ☆

Question #200: What is the Sofer?

ה: The couch on which Jews traditionally recline after the Passover seder.

ב: The nickname used for the Zefat (Safed) Rebbe.

ג: The scribe who writes the Torah scroll and other religious documents.

ד: The name of the prayer book used on Tisha B'av.

ה: The pen used by the bride and groom to sign the ketubah.

☆ ☆ ☆ ☆ ☆ ☆ ☆ ☆ ☆ ☆ ☆ ☆ ☆ ☆ ☆ ☆ ☆

Question #201: What is Karpas?

ה: The meal which breaks the fast after Yom Kippur.

ב: The blessing recited before eating meat.

ג: The ceremonial slaying of the carp prior to the preparation of gefilte fish.

ד: The green vegetable served during the Passover seder, symbolizing rebirth and spring.

ה: A toll tag system for Israeli cars to avoid stopping to pay tolls on the Jerusalem-Tel Aviv highway.

Answers: #196 - ג   #197 - ב   #198 - ה

Question #202: Who invented the Polaroid Land camera?

א: Jonathan Pollard.

ב: Edwin Land.

ג: John Cameron Swayze.

ד: Michael Landon.

ה: Yaakov Minolta.

✡ ✡ ✡ ✡ ✡ ✡ ✡ ✡ ✡ ✡ ✡ ✡ ✡ ✡ ✡ ✡ ✡ ✡ ✡

Question #203: What is Kavanah?

א: The kapital of Kuba.

ב: The congregation.

ג: One's personal feelings or response in prayer.

ד: The ceremony of lifting the Torah.

ה: A mystical belief that the soul of the deceased will return to Jerusalem when the Messiah comes.

✡ ✡ ✡ ✡ ✡ ✡ ✡ ✡ ✡ ✡ ✡ ✡ ✡ ✡ ✡ ✡ ✡ ✡

Question #204: What is Naturai Karta?

א: The nude beach north of Tel Aviv.

ב: In biblical times, the aqueduct which carried water to Jerusalem from the Jordan River.

ג: The milk cart which was pushed by Tevye in the Spanish version of *Fiddler On The Roof.*

ד: The Israeli version of the Sierra Club.

ה: An ultra orthodox group which does not recognize the state of Israel.

Question #205: What is Sheitel?

ה: The black hat worn by Chassidim.

ב: Tevye's oldest daughter.

ג: The covering over a Torah scroll.

ד: A wig, worn as a head covering by religious married women.

ה: The swaying motion made by Jews in prayer.

✧ ✧ ✧ ✧ ✧ ✧ ✧ ✧ ✧ ✧ ✧ ✧ ✧ ✧ ✧ ✧ ✧ ✧ ✧

Question #206: What is Midrash?

ה: A skin disease common in the ancient Middle East.

ב: A popular mode of dress among Israeli teenage girls, wherein the pupik is exposed.

ג: A method of interpreting scripture through stories or homilies.

ד: The collected commentaries of Rashi.

ה: The collection of writings by the priests of ancient Israel.

✧ ✧ ✧ ✧ ✧ ✧ ✧ ✧ ✧ ✧ ✧ ✧ ✧ ✧ ✧ ✧ ✧ ✧

Question #207: Who founded the movement known as "The Theatre Of The Absurd"?

ה: Eugene Ionesco.

ב: Neil Simon.

ג: Robin Williams.

ד: Marcel Marceau.

ה: Joe Rogan.

Answers: #202 - ב   *#203 -* ג   *#204 -* ה

Question #208: What is Saboraim?

א: These were the followers of Shammai.

ב: A group of scholars in Babylonia, responsible for much of the Talmud.

ג: A hair condition common in the dry desert region of the Middle East.

ד: Refers to the priests who were assigned the task of performing sacrifices at the Temple in Jerusalem.

ה: Jews who secretly maintained observance of the Sabbath during the Inquisition.

✡ ✡ ✡ ✡ ✡ ✡ ✡ ✡ ✡ ✡ ✡ ✡ ✡ ✡ ✡ ✡ ✡ ✡

Question #209: Who wrote "The Naked And The Dead"?

א: Philip Roth.

ב: Erica Jong.

ג: Norman Mailer.

ד: Gypsy Rose Lee.

ה: Steven Page and Jerry Garcia.

✡ ✡ ✡ ✡ ✡ ✡ ✡ ✡ ✡ ✡ ✡ ✡ ✡ ✡ ✡ ✡ ✡ ✡

Question #210: What is the Gaza Strip?

א: A portion of land along the Mediterranean coast captured by Israel in the Six Day War.

ב: Refers to the "no man's land" between Israel and Lebanon.

ג: The airport which serves the Sinai Desert.

ד: A Middle Eastern poker game.

ה: A Middle Eastern belly dance.

Answers: #205 - **ד**   *#206 -* **ג**   *#207 -* **א**

Question #211: Who provided the voice of Charlie the Tuna?

א: Salmon Rushdie.

ב: Eddie Fisher.

ג: Zero Mostel.

ד: Jackie Mason.

ה: Hershel Bernardi.

✧ ✧ ✧ ✧ ✧ ✧ ✧ ✧ ✧ ✧ ✧ ✧ ✧ ✧ ✧ ✧ ✧ ✧ ✧

Question #212: What is Sh'chach?

א: The sound made by a Jew who is choking.

ב: An Israeli political party which is opposed to territorial compromise with the Arabs.

ג: The branches placed on the roof of a sukkah.

ד: A nonsense word used in Israeli kindergartens when teaching children how to pronounce the letters chet and chof.

ה: The fourth month of the Jewish calendar.

✧ ✧ ✧ ✧ ✧ ✧ ✧ ✧ ✧ ✧ ✧ ✧ ✧ ✧ ✧ ✧ ✧ ✧

Question #213: What is the movie "Cast a Giant Shadow" about?

א: The impact of the anti-Zionist religious parties in Israel on modern Israeli politics.

ב: The biography of Lamont Cranston.

ג: It is about the building of the Al Aqsa mosque on the Temple Mount in Jerusalem.

ד: The building of the Shalom Tower in Tel Aviv, the largest skyscraper in Israel.

ה: U. S. Army Colonel Mickey Marcus, who played a major role in the Israeli army during the country's founding.

Answers: #208 - ב #209 - ג #210 - א

Question #214: What was the Balfour Declaration?

א: The declaration by the First Zionist Congress in Basle that a Jewish state will be established in Palestine.

ב: The declaration by British prime minister Arthur Balfour in 1948 that Great Britain recognizes the new state of Israel.

ג: The declaration by the British government that it supports the establishment of a Jewish state in Palestine.

ד: The declaration by the chief umpire of Israel that a batter can walk when receiving four balls.

ה: The declaration by the new government of Israel in 1948 that anyone Jewish can return to Israel and claim citizenship.

✡ ✡ ✡ ✡ ✡ ✡ ✡ ✡ ✡ ✡ ✡ ✡ ✡ ✡ ✡ ✡ ✡ ✡ ✡

Question #215: In North Carolina, Rabbi Harold Friedman used a vehicle as a mobile congregation. What was this vehicle called?

א: The Harley Magen Davidson.

ב: The Circuit Riding Rabbi Bus.

ג: The Rebbe's Winnebagle.

ד: The Mitzvah Mobile.

ה: The Rebbe Humvee.

✡ ✡ ✡ ✡ ✡ ✡ ✡ ✡ ✡ ✡ ✡ ✡ ✡ ✡ ✡ ✡ ✡ ✡ ✡

Question #216: What was the Auto-da-fe?

א: The first car manufactured in Israel.

ב: The public sentencing of Jews and other heretics during the Inquisition.

ג: The Sephardic version of Kol Nidre, when one atones and affirms his faith in G-d.

ד: A self-service restaurant chain in Israel.

ה: The annual Israeli road rally competition.

Answers: #211 - ה   #212 - ג   #213 - ה

Question #217: Who were Zechariah and Zephaniah?

א: Two kings of Judea.

ב: Two of the minor prophets.

ג: A championship World Wrestling Federation tag team.

ד: The famous "twin prophets of doom," who both wrote of the coming destruction of the Jewish people because of their sins.

ה: Two bullfrogs mentioned in the story of the ten plagues.

✿ ✿ ✿ ✿ ✿ ✿ ✿ ✿ ✿ ✿ ✿ ✿ ✿ ✿ ✿ ✿ ✿ ✿

Question #218: What is Sheva Berakhot?

א: A blessing recited when seven good things happen in one day.

ב: The blessing over a new Chevrolet car.

ג: The seven blessings, recited at a wedding.

ד: The blessing said when entering the city of Be'er Sheva in Israel.

ה: The traditional prayers recited by mourners.

✿ ✿ ✿ ✿ ✿ ✿ ✿ ✿ ✿ ✿ ✿ ✿ ✿ ✿ ✿ ✿ ✿ ✿

Question #219: For what was Baba Rabbah known?

א: He was a disciple of Rambam who wrote extensively on the importance of penitence.

ב: He codified what became known as the Babylonian Talmud.

ג: This was a character played by Gilda Radner on *Saturday Night Live*.

ד: He was the father of Ali Baba (of Forty Thieves fame).

ה: He was a Samaritan high priest in the fourth century who led the fight for freedom against the Romans.

Answers: #214 - **ג**   *#215 -* **ב**   *#216 -* **ב**

✿ ✿ ✿ ✿ ✿ ✿ ✿ ✿ ✿ ✿ ✿ ✿ ✿ ✿ ✿ ✿ ✿ ✿ ✿

VISIT US AT

http://www.zimcocreativearts.com

✿ ✿ ✿ ✿ ✿ ✿ ✿ ✿ ✿ ✿ ✿ ✿ ✿ ✿ ✿ ✿ ✿ ✿ ✿